Third Printing
March 2014

ISBN 978-0-9892191-0-5

PRINTED IN THE UNITED STATES OF AMERICA
Printed by

Advertiser Printers, Inc.
320 Clay Street
Dayton, KY 41074
800-354-9707

Dedication

"Daniel's life has touched more lives than ours ever could.
We just marvel at the things God has allowed Daniel to do,
and the wonderful people he has met.
We want these people to see not only Daniel,
but more importantly, his astonishing God.
This book will help us, especially Daniel,
tell people about his God.
That's what Daniel wants, and those are the
folks to whom we dedicate our story."

The Stratman Family

To God the Father, God the Son,
and God the Holy Spirit, my One
and All, my Everything - pleasing
You is my deepest heart's desire.
May You be glorified!

Heart-Felt Acknowledgments

To my laid-back, quiet-spirited husband, Tom, whose unflagging devotion and servant heart help me believe God truly does champion me and cheer-lead me,

I dedicate this book.

To my children, grandchildren, and family – gifts immeasurable from my Heavenly Father.

To my life-long mentors, Kenny and Ethel Hitch - God knew I couldn't make it without you in my life.

To Sue Wade, whose words to me, "You were made to write!" gave me vision to stay the course.

To Freddy Bollinger, who reads almost everything I write, and enthusiastically tells me how much it blesses her and will bless others.

To Mickey Wiggershaus, who walks with me on the mountaintop and in the pit.

To Gail Frost, a "silver" friend who feels like "gold".

To my almost-life-long craft group sisters - you are God's Hands and Heart to me.

To our "couple-friends" - John and Freddy Bollinger, Bob and Ruth Cload, Karen and Lonnie Crisp, Ro and Garywayne Dennison, Don and Gail Frost, Skip and Linda Holmes, Joe and Alice Robb, Bob and Sue Wade, Dennis and Lorena Wampler, Mark and Mickey Wiggershaus - like Moses, we need you to prop up our arms.

To my Monday morning and Thursday afternoon prayer groups and Judy Jordon - you lift me up on wings of prayer so I have strength to serve Him Whom my heart loves. To our Sunday evening Shepherd Group - you are spiritual family, a safe place where we can grow and be blessed.

Ecclesiastes 1:9 tells us, "What has been will be again, what has been done will be done again; there is nothing new under the sun." My entire life has been spent "soaking up" the wisdom of God's Word and that of thousands of others whose lives and writings have influenced my life. With gratitude, I acknowledge their contributions to my life and to my writing.

Foreword by Joni Eareckson Tada

I've gotten used to being on display. Whether it's the child studying my wheelchair, the elderly gent across the way smiling sympathetically, or the waiter eyeing me carefully as I use my bent-spoon to eat spaghetti, I'm aware that people are watching. Some might watch out of pity, some out of admiration. I sense that all watch with unspoken questions.

It's what Daniel Stratman faces every day. Years ago a botched operation severely damaged his motor skills, eyesight, and ability to speak, and so, yes, he draws a few stares. But like Daniel, I choose to think that people's unspoken questions are well intended. That's because this young man and I, as followers of Jesus Christ, are constrained to think the best of others. We are called to be on display (as any Christian is). We are encouraged by God's Word to smile from the inside-out as the strength of the Lord shows up bountifully through our physical limitations. When people watch Daniel persevere to speak, get excited about a Cardinals game, crack jokes (sometimes with great effort), and walk with his halting gait, well … I believe they're thinking, "How great his God must be to inspire such faith and confidence."

Daniel and Joni at Family Retreat

Somehow, I don't think Daniel minds being on display. His story inspires faith and confidence in people who observe him – and his remarkable family, too. I remember the first time I saw Daniel back in the 1990's – he and his family had come to Los Angeles for medical help and had stopped by the office of Joni and Friends for a visit. I was struck by Daniel's winsome sense of humor, his warm smile, and sunlit confidence in Christ. As we conversed (because talking to Daniel takes time), I found him to be like any other good-looking young college-bound kid. I told him he looked like someone in a "Brooks Brothers" advertisement. A few weeks later a bottle of Brooks Brothers cologne arrived in the mail!

To spend time with Daniel is to hardly notice the fact that he has a significant disability. His happy-hearted disposition bolsters the spirits of everyone around him. I should know. Daniel and the entire Stratman family have participated in many of our Joni and Friends Family Retreats, and everywhere he goes, people are drawn to him. The young man whose story you hold in your hands may be lacking 'typical' use of legs and hands, but I find it ironic that God should use such a person to move the rest of us to step out to touch and embrace others.

Daniel Stratman spent seven years inspiring the lives of countless students on the campus of Emmaus Bible College … the college from which he recently graduated. And nothing could please me more than to have this excellent book published which, I know, will inspire a new generation – not only on campus, but across the country. It's all about inspiration. It's all about encouragement.

This is what will strike you about When Losing Is Winning. In a world that is splitting apart at the seams, we need to hear from courageous people who can extend the grace of God through their stories of hope and healing. The Stratman family does that … and more. They are very ordinary, yet so extraordinary. And like me, you will think, *If Daniel can, by the grace of God, overcome his limitations, I can, too.*

Joni Eareckson Tada
Agoura Hills, California

Joni and the Stratman family

Introduction

My attention was arrested by a young man in a wheelchair sitting not more than ten feet across the room from me. Like a magnet, my mind seemed riveted to him; I couldn't tear my eyes away. We were in the middle of a worship service, and I struggled to regain composure, to place my focus back on the God my heart so dearly loved and desperately needed. Yet I couldn't turn from the young man in his chair. I had not noticed him before.

We were at a Joni and Friends Family Retreat, the third day into the five we were to spend together at Lake Wawasee in Syracuse, Indiana, at the Oakwood Inn. It was my sixth retreat serving as a volunteer, together with a hundred-and-fifteen other volunteers who had been called by the Spirit of God, sent to serve the fifty-plus families who had come to the Inn for respite and relief, restoration and recreation.

I knew why my mind and heart were riveted to the young man in his wheelchair. The turn of his jaw, the smoothness of his young, freshly shaven cheek, the hairline that caressed his forehead - I had seen them all before even though I had never previously encountered this particular young man. They were the same as those I had last seen on my own beautiful son, twelve years earlier, as they ushered me from the room so they could close the casket which took his beloved, nineteen-year-old body from my grief-worn eyes for the last time on this pain-filled, groaning earth.

Matthew was a child with severe special needs, God's gift to my husband and me through adoption. At fifteen days of age, thirty-one years earlier, the social worker had placed him in our arms. Our hearts burgeoned with some of the sweetest, most poignant feelings we had yet experienced. With our numerous human failings and many parental inadequacies, for nineteen years we loved and cherished our sweet and troubled son as best we knew how, watching him grow, astonished at the many miracles God granted us relative to his young life as it unfolded in our family. And now, twelve years after we had left his drug-battered body at his graveside, I saw that familiar jaw and hairline once again, that beloved curve of the cheek, in the profile of this beautiful young man across the room. And I knew by the drawing of my heart and spirit that God had a plan for my immediate future that included this young man and his family. His name was Daniel Stratman.

Two years later my husband Tom and I flew to Iowa to spend three lovely days interviewing and taping Jay, Susan, and Daniel Stratman. What a joyful, faith-building time! Daniel and his family are eager for this book to be written. Susan explains, "Daniel's life has touched more lives than mine ever could. I just marvel at the things Daniel has done and the people he has met. I want these people to see not only Daniel, but more importantly, his astonishing God. This book will help us, especially Daniel, tell people about God. That's what Daniel wants."

What better gift could we give anyone than to introduce them to our God Who comforts us when we're grieving, rests us when we're weary, forgives us when we're guilt-ridden, motivates and gives us power to change our lives as needed, and freely gives us abundant joy and eternal bliss?

What you will read herein follows two primary paths. Path one contains the events of the story as they unfold in the lives of the Stratman Family. Path two contains specific glimpses into Who our glorious God is as the story breaks them open and reveals Him. I have deliberately capitalized references to God to emphasize His power and presence in our lives. I have deliberately refrained from capitalizing references to satan.

What you will read is written to bless you, to encourage and exhort you, to comfort you when you weep and to double your joys, to God's glory. May the words dance off the page and into your heart!

Table of Contents

PART THREE

"Now to him who is able to do immeasurably more than all we ask or imagine, according to his power that is at work within us..."
Eph. 3:20

CHAPTER I

The Valley Of Death's Shadow

"Our family verse has always been Eph. 3:20," said Susan, in the note she penned to me in January of 2006. Little did she know, eleven years previously, how that verse would help hold the gates of hell at bay as they threatened to close in on her and her family on that tragic day in 1996.

On October 17, 1984, at the precise time appointed by our compassionate, sovereign God, Daniel Lee Stratman, via Caesarian section, made his grand entrance into the family of Jay (35), Susan (30), Jayme (3-1/2), and Jodie (1-1/2) Stratman. The celebration began! With tears of joy streaming down faces filled with gratitude and glee, Jay and Susan together agreed, "Jayme will be thrilled to have a brother!"

Years before Daniel's birth, Jay had chosen the name he wanted for his son, should God graciously grant him such a gift. Daniel Smith, Jay's professor and president of Emmaus Bible College, was a godly mentor whom Jay admired as well as emulated. He was a worthy namesake for his baby boy.

Jay wanted a son for numerous reasons, one of which was to share with him his spectator's love of sports. As a child, Jay enjoyed attending baseball games with his father and brothers, and hoped to carry on that tradition with his son. Jay's dream would eventually materialize, most assuredly and quite delightfully, but not in the way that Jay envisioned it in 1984.

Within hours, the celebration over the news of the birth of a baby boy was dramatically tempered. In recovery, a doctor told

Susan and Jay their son had been born with a "significant heart murmur, not the kind that goes away". The doctor said that because Daniel was not blue, and was breathing on his own, the medical staff was not concerned. But they were going to "keep an eye on him". Jay and Susan would need to take him to a cardiologist sometime during his first month of life.

Shortly thereafter Susan knew that, despite what the doctor said, there was indeed something about which to be concerned. The nurses were bringing other babies on the hospital floor to their mothers to be fed, but they rarely brought in Daniel. When they did, Daniel would nurse for a few seconds and fall asleep. The nurses would unbundle him and sprinkle his feet and head with water to waken him, but Daniel just wasn't interested. Because he weighed in at eight-and-a-half pounds, the nurses were unperturbed, saying some babies were just lazy, and Daniel could "feed off the fat of the land". But mothers have a God-ordained intuition about their children, and it soon became evident to Susan that something was terribly wrong. Daniel slept his entire second night without waking or eating, a behavior Susan recognized as ominously atypical of newborns. Susan cried, read Psalms from the Bible, and cried some more. Past experience had shown her that, as a chronic worrier plagued with various "what-if's" and sundry fears, she could find peace in God's Word in the midst of those fears.

The next day Susan's concern prompted agreement to an x-ray, which revealed nothing unusual.

Five days after Daniel's birth, they were discharged from the hospital with a second reminder to call a cardiologist within a month because the murmur was "very loud". Before leaving the hospital, Susan called their family pediatrician. The urgency in her mother's heart and the fear in her voice convinced the receptionist to tell Susan to bring Daniel in that very day.

Dr. Baker immediately perceived that Daniel was dying of heart failure, his organs already enlarged. He called Children's Hospital and immediately sent them to the emergency room, where a heart team was waiting for them.

Upon arrival, a nurse checked Daniel's blood pressure and commented, "This blood pressure cuff is not working". She tried another one and again remarked, "I don't know what the deal is, but this one's not working either". At that moment, the cardiologist, Dr. Birahah, walked in, took one look at Daniel's chest rising and falling in labored breathing, and said, "The blood pressure cuffs are fine. This baby's dying!"

Thus began the first of numerous walks through the "valley of the shadow of death" with Daniel Lee Stratman, the advent of a laborious and prolonged process of learning to lay him down, and the conscious beginning of a gradual, deeper *knowing* of a God Who loves us beyond our ability to perceive that love.

Our God Who Calms Our Fears

"Past experience had shown her that, as a chronic worrier...,she could find peace in God's Word in the midst of those fears."

Susan knew, from her long history of struggling with fear, exactly where to turn when her heart hurt and her spirit sagged. There was only One Who could minister to her soul, rout her fear and restore her strength. When her heart fainted, she had previous experience with the "Lifter-of-her-head" (Ps. 3:3). She had encounters with her God of Ps. 34:4, "I sought the Lord, and He answered me; He delivered me from all my fears." She didn't fight her spiritual battle alone, nor do we, nor did the Bible folks we read of in God's Word. In Ps. 138 we hear David's testimony that God stayed close to him in his fear, made him bold and stout-hearted (inflexible to temptation) when he cried out for Him. Timothy's testimony is similar - the Lord stood with him, strengthened him, and rescued him from every evil attack (2 Tim. 4:17a, 18a). Susan's testimony is the same.

When we are deeply frightened, when fear fills us with dread and alarm, paralyzes us, robs our joy and renders us impotent, we don't have the strength or inner resources needed to throw it off, to keep our head above the water-line. And so God intentionally makes it very clear in His Word that He not only stands by us, He also fights FOR us. In Ex. 14:14 He tells us we need only to be still, because He will do the fighting. He promises to work in us to banish our spirit of fear, to cause us to stand firm in Christ. He leads us in triumphal procession against fear or any other temptation that rises up against us. Hallelujah! (Phil. 2:13, 2 Cor. 1:21a, 2 Cor. 2:14a).

God understands about fainting hearts. His Son Jesus had one in Gethsemane. Jesus hurt so bad He needed His friends to stand by Him, stay near Him, and hold Him up in prayer while He wrestled with His pain. His heart was so heavy with sorrow He wasn't sure He would live through it. The anguish of His agony expressed itself in earnest pleading for His Father to remove His suffering, release Him from the intense pain of soul, body, and spirit. Such was the compelling depth of Jesus' pain that this Son, Who spent His entire life delighting in the doing of His Father's will, dared to approach Him three times seeking a reprieve.

His Father understood. He sent no reprimand, no preaching words, no simplistic reassurances. He sent an angel to minister to Jesus, to help Him, to strengthen His dear Son.

In 2 Tim. 1:7, God tells us clearly He has not given us a spirit of fear. He loves us, calls us His friends, and wants for us only those things that are good (Is. 43:4, John 15:13-15, Ps. 119:68a). God has given us a spirit of courage, love, and a sound mind; He is our God who calms our fears. He does that, as Susan says, through and by His Word. "He keepeth him in perfect peace whose mind is stayed on Him, because he trusts in Him." (Is. 26:3). By God's grace and by setting our faces like flint we keep our thoughts focused on God's Word and Person. Reading Psalms aloud and speaking verses we have memorized and hidden in our hearts, such as Is. 26:3 and Is. 41:10, routs our worst fears, robs satan of his potential power over us, restores our peace, and allows us access to the spirit of courage, love, and sound mind God has given us. We discover, as we keep our minds on Him, He is indeed our God Who Calms Our Fears. Thank You, Lord.

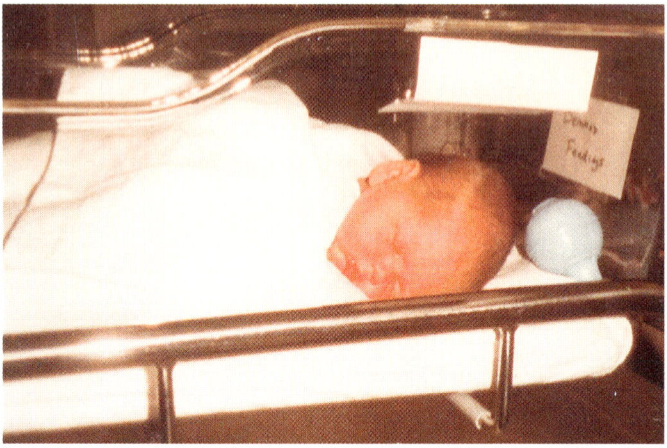

Daniel — 5 days old

Bright-eyed at age 2 years

"The earth is the LORD'S, and everything in it, the world, and all who live in it." Ps. 24:1

CHAPTER 2

Laying Daniel Down

Dr. Birahah offered the Stratmans little hope for Daniel's life. "I don't really think he's going to make it through the night. Daniel will probably not live through the next two or three hours. We're going to call someone else to come in to consult, and do what we can do."

"At the doctor's words, the floor opened up and gobbled us down," said Susan. "Our world turned upside down. We were horrified. We stumbled to the phone booth and called my Mom, who called her prayer chain and our prayer chain at church, as well as our pastor."

"When we returned to the emergency room the surgeon told us he would try to do a catheterization to see exactly what was wrong inside Daniel's little body. If he survived the catheterization, they would operate accordingly, but they couldn't do the surgery at Children's Hospital." Barnes-Jewish Hospital was connected to Children's via long corridors. They put Daniel on a gurney. Jay and Susan, five days after her Cesarean Section delivery, literally ran behind the gurney as Daniel was briskly transferred to Barnes-Jewish.

"Daniel made it through the catheterization. They told us he had aortic stenosis. His aortic valve was deformed and had closed. Blood and oxygen were not getting to his body. He was a new-born, his organs were enlarged, he was already so compromised they didn't think he'd make it through surgery, but they were going to operate immediately anyway."

"Several friends were at the hospital with us by this time. Surgery began at 10:00 p.m. Someone came out periodically to tell us how things were going, and at 12:30 a.m. the surgeon walked into the waiting room with a smile on his face. He said things went very well, and Daniel was stable. They had performed microscopic surgery and cut the aortic valve open, cutting little snips to make it a tricuspid valve. It wasn't working properly, but it was working."

"I remember the tears pouring down my face, the immense relief flooding through my body. It almost seemed as if none of the past several hours had really happened. They seemed like a blur, a bad dream, a nightmare. I sat in my chair and I sang. I just sang, the words pouring out of my soul. *How can I give thanks for the things You have done for me? Things so undeserved, yet You came to prove Your love to me? To God be the glory for the things He has done!"*[2]

"Earlier, when Jay and I stumbled outside to the phone booth to call my Mom, we were a wreck. I remember Jay telling me 'Sue, we need to give him back to God.' So we stood in front of that phone booth and cried out our hearts to God. 'Lord, we love this little boy so much already. But He's Yours. If you want to take him back, we give him to You. We understand. We'll be okay because You'll help us be okay. He's Yours, and we give our only son back to You.' We stood there hugging each other, sobbing, just sobbing."

Susan and Jay laid their Daniel down. How gently, how unremittingly, how unflaggingly our God, Who desires nothing more than He desires our fellowship with Him, pursues us on the path toward intimacy with Him. He knows that He has made us for Himself. He knows our deepest joy and greatest satisfaction lie in Him. In His presence is the fullness of our joy. At His right Hand are our eternal pleasures (Ps. 16:11). But in the way that is common to human beings, we look elsewhere for our delights, our fulfillment, our thrills. And they all prove to be fragile shells, lovely on the outside, empty on the inside, able to provide only a fleeting measure of satisfaction that fades and crumbles, as do all earthly things. As in Abraham's life with Isaac (Gen. 21), they distract our attention, absorb our hearts, and become our idols, to our great detriment. We become dependent on them instead of God, without realizing we are so doing. God has to pry our fingers off of them. Charles Spurgeon claims that favorite children and spouses are often the cause of much sin and pain in our lives. God is grieved when He sees us "doting on them above measure".[3]

It's testimony to our forgetfulness that we even consider "giving back" to God someone or something that has never truly been ours, but has always and will always belong to the God Who created all things. (Ps. 24). King David and the leaders of Israel were conscious of the irony therein. They had given wholeheartedly and extravagantly of their personal treasuries to God, and found great joy in so doing. Yet in the midst of that rejoicing they experienced a profound awareness that everything they had just given to God to build His temple had first been given to them by Him. David finds it a humbling proposition. "But who am I, and who are my people, that we should be able to give as generously as this? Everything comes from You, and we have given You only what comes from Your Hand" (1 Chr. 29:14). Yet that giving back is exactly what God wants from us. It pleases Him when we lay our Daniels down.

As in the life of Abraham, God preserved sweet Daniel's life. He remained ten days in the hospital with no set-backs; then was joyfully and gratefully taken home, bringing to closure the first of many occasions wherein Jay and Susan would be asked to lay their Daniel down.

Our God Who Cries With Us

"We stood there hugging each other, sobbing, just sobbing."

God is not made in our image. We are made in His image, i.e., God cries. The Scriptures are clear - God reveals Himself to us as One Who weeps. Jesus wept with Martha and Mary at Lazarus' tomb, and again as His heart anguished over the coming destruction of His beloved inhabitants of Jerusalem (Lk. 19:41).

Jesus wept with Susan and Jay as they anguished over Daniel. He weeps with you and with me as we agonize over our griefs and pains. We can count on it. That's just Who He is, a compassionate God Who enters into our woundedness, a tender God Who comforts us "As a loving mother comforts her child, so will I comfort you;… (Is. 66:13).

David, the man whom the Holy Spirit identifies as one who had captured God's heart, wrote of his God as One Who was intensely interested in every detail of David's life. David was confident that his God had a special, particular concern for his pains and, more specifically, his every tear. What soothing comfort is available to our broken hearts as we read the reassuring words in Ps. 56:8 that speak of God as recording David's laments, caring enough about his anguish to not just notice or observe, but to write it down. He puts the tears David cries in a bottle, saves them and cherishes them. The Hebrew word *nodah* is translated as a skin or leather bag for fluids, or a bottle. Taken literally or metaphorically, it is an incredibly moving description of our personal God Who cries with us. And, it is an intentional and purposeful revelation of God, and from God, about Who He is and His deep love for us.

Even when we weep because we have sinned, as a result of doing the wrong thing, and are experiencing the consequences of our own selfish choices, when God corrects and curbs us He does not do so gleefully or "willingly". He corrects us and disciplines us to turn us back to what is best for us, back to Himself where we are happiest, yet it grieves Him to administer that discipline. Lam. 3:32,33 reminds us of His great heart for us, His unquenchable love toward us. "Though He brings grief, He will show compassion, so great is His unfailing love. For He does not willingly bring affliction or grief to the children of men." God lays this truth out for us to clearly see in I Chr. 21 wherein David sins by ordering a count of his troops even after God has warned him against doing so through his army captain Joab. Joab pleads with David not to bring sin-guilt on Israel. But David's authority overrules Joab, and David orders a troop count anyway.

After he chooses to sin, God confronts him for doing so, and in His great mercy allows David to choose the form of discipline to be administered.

David is no proverbial "dummy". Of three options, he chooses the one God will directly administer Himself. David has a long history with God. He knows God's character includes unreasonable and radical mercy as well as reasonable and conservative justice. Even as He is administering David's discipline, God's great compassion curbs and actually aborts it while it is in process. God is grieved as He watches the calamity occurring, and stops the destroying angel as he works. Our hearts melt at the thought of a sinless, supreme God Whose Heart is so very tender toward us.

David knew God brought affliction only for David's good. "Before I was afflicted, I went astray, but now I obey Your Word... It was good for me to be afflicted so that I might learn Your decrees" (Ps. 119:67, 71).

In Jer. 31:13 God promises, "For I will turn their mourning into joy, and will comfort them, and make them rejoice after their sorrow." God does this even for those of us who lay down our sons and find He has chosen not to restore them as He restored Isaac to Abraham and Daniel to the Stratmans. As God weeps with us and comforts those whose children are taken home to heaven before their parents are, He heals our hearts and souls. He makes us whole again. Weeping <u>does</u> remain for a night, but joy <u>does</u> come in the morning, at the Hands of our God Who Cries With Us. Thank You, Lord.

Daniel with sisters Jodie (2) and Jayme (4).

Daniel 2 months old

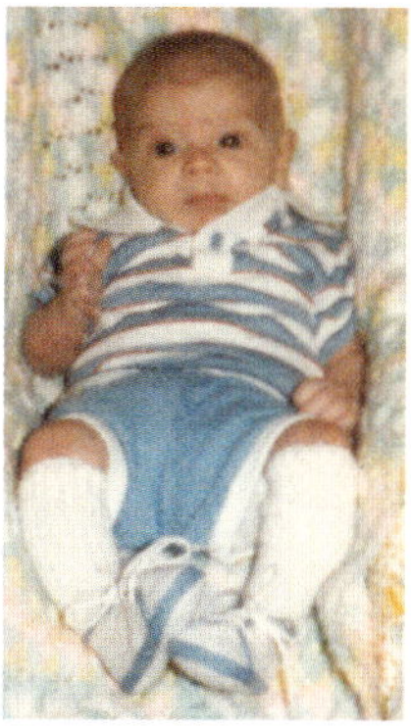

"...Jesus...said, 'This sickness will not end in death, ...it is for God's glory...'" John 11:4

CHAPTER 3

Why, Lord?

"There were so many questions running around in my head during those initial days Daniel spent in the hospital," says Susan. "We did not have a friend or a family member who had a child in the hospital. We didn't even know anyone who had a child with a long-term illness. Everyone we knew had healthy children. And so, of course, the questions hammered and gnawed at me. 'Why us, God? Why did You allow this to happen to us? What sin is in my life?' I thought it must all be my fault. I wasn't angry with God, because it wasn't God's fault, it was mine. I wanted to know what I had done, what I should have done differently. What had I not learned that I should have learned?"

"And, of course, satan kept plaguing me with thoughts about my lack of trust. I feared almost everything. I wasn't able to give things to the Lord and leave them there. I would give them to Him, then take them back, thinking I needed to help Him solve the problem. It was a vicious cycle. And I was a mess!"

"Jay wasn't that way. He had trust and faith in God that I didn't have. He wasn't a worrier; he was solid in his beliefs."

"As Daniel turned a year old I got pregnant with his younger sister. I was terrified. The Lord came to my aid before I was even certain I was indeed pregnant. He soothed and reassured me with Is. 40:11, "He will gently lead those who are with young." But I did not accept His aid. When Daniel was born the doctors at the hospital told us our chances of having other children with congenital defects were greater since we already had one. I let myself get all worked up again, caught up in the 'what-ifs'. I was definitely not happy with this pregnancy! Probably more than I realized, I was still living with raw nerves and unsettled emotions. I just cringed at the thought of another baby and our family again going through what Daniel had been through."

Daniel progressed normally during his first year of life. He walked at nine months, with no physical delays in his development. Every three months Susan and Jay took him to Children's Hospital for a heart check. Those were grueling, anxiety-ridden trips. Twenty-five-years ago, most babies with defects like Daniel's simply died. The technology necessary to operate on those tiny valves was not available. There was a constant, nagging awareness that if the check-up uncovered a closed valve again, the doctors were unsure as to how they would proceed.

"I went back to the obstetrician who had delivered Daniel. He knew, of course, about Daniel's heart defect. He suggested we could terminate the pregnancy. I told him abortion was not an option, and he insisted it was. When I stood solid on my position, he became very rude to me from that point on."

"I left the office extremely upset, more so than when I entered it. I felt alone. The paralyzing fears had returned. I remember driving across the Missouri River on the St. Charles Bridge, thinking how easy it would be to just do a quick turn, go over the bridge, and be done. No more anxiety, stress or pain. I had been in a panic mode when I entered the obstetrician's office. That had not changed. I walked out of his office crying and got in my car crying. I remember trying so hard to focus on the verse, 'Whenever I feel afraid, I will trust in You.' Over and over I repeated it" (Ps. 56:3).

"When I got home I was still crying. I was literally falling apart. Jay took us all for a ride – it was Saturday, so he had stayed home to care for the children. When we got in the car, God used the children's 'Psalty' tape to calm me down. The words of the song they were playing are:

'I will cast all my cares upon You.
I lay all my burdens down at Your feet,
and anytime I don't know what to do,
I will cast all my cares upon You.'[4]

The Lord used that song to get me to stop worrying, at least for the moment. I periodically found myself fretting again, but the words to that song would get my focus back on trusting God. It became my theme song. He used it to encourage me. He always gives me what I need! He is so faithful!"

Susan changed obstetricians, and when she came out of her new doctor's office the next week, she was no longer unhappy about her pregnancy. Susan says her new doctor, recommended by a friend, was "fabulous". He ordered an ultrasound which showed the baby was developing normally. Jay suggested they name their "in-utero" little girl "Joy", because that's what they needed to focus on. Susan agreed!

Our God Who Disciplines

"Why, God? Why did You allow this to happen to us? What sin is in my life?"

Susan thought what many people think; there were no options in her mind. She was at fault, and the reason for Daniel's difficulties lay within her; God was disciplining her.

But God says that's not always true. Sometimes, it is true, what we suffer is due to the sin in our own life. Sometimes God uses our difficulties as a wake-up call, to alert us to the things we need to change. But that's not always so.

In His Word, His love letter to us, God tells us pain and suffering occur for three basic reasons. Two are set forth in John 11 in the beautifully tender account of Lazarus' death and resurrection. Jesus says in 11:4 that sickness (suffering) may be unto death. It may be the route we have to take in our fallen world to arrive in heaven. He also says it may not be so; it may be sickness for the purpose of God's glory. In verse 45 we learn that many of the Jews who saw what Jesus did when He raised Lazarus from the dead put their faith in Him, believed in Him. Jesus was glorified thereby.

In Job 5:17,18, and in numerous other Scripture verses, God sets forth His third reason for difficulties and suffering. "Praise the Lord! Happy is the man whom God corrects! So do not despise the disciplines of the Almighty, for He wounds, but He also binds up. He injures, but His Hand also heals." We can be sure, in that deep down place of absolute certainty inside of us, that God will never fail to bind up and heal any corrective wounds He delivers. Unlike human beings, He will never, ever leave us in our woundedness. He will walk with us through it, carry us when necessary and, when we have learned what we needed to learn for our own growth and good, He will deliver us from it (Is. 46:4). Pain and beauty seem to be the two things that touch our lives most deeply. Pain's fire melts the ice that hardens the clay of our souls. It opens our spirit to God's will. It takes us to the bottom of our being, and once we have been there, we find that it is solid ground, because He is there. While satan sends us pain and tribulation to cause us to stumble, God sends pain and tribulation to cause us to stand.

In reality, the very fact that God bothers to discipline and correct us at all is undeniable evidence of His deep love and care for us. "My son, do not despise the Lord's discipline, and do not resent His rebuke, because the Lord disciplines those He loves, as a father (disciplines) the son in whom He delights" (Prov. 3:11). God is not so much interested in our comfort as in our character, nor in our happiness as in our holiness.

Quite different from suffering or discipline that's linked to the sin in our lives is suffering that is connected to our deep love and devotion to Him Who is our All-in-All. Often those folks of greatest devotion seem to know the deepest darkness. In that darkness we don't really need an explanation; we need God. Sometimes we don't know the why in order that we might better know the Who. Where reason cannot wade, faith must swim. Relationship with our God carries us through. He identifies Himself as our Very Great Reward, and indeed He is.

Paul <u>wanted</u> to know Christ and the fellowship of sharing in His suffering (Phil. 3:10). Paul knew that sharing in anyone's suffering, especially Christ's, deepens our intimacy with that person. Suffering deepens our capacity for God, for relationship with Him. Because we fail to realize or appreciate the unspeakable treasure of experiencing Jesus in the fellowship of His suffering, we resist it, retreat from it, resent it, rebuke it, and sometimes throw a pity party as Job did in chapters 10, 11, and 40:8. In failing to recognize suffering as an opportunity to die to self, to be freed from self-bondage and self-absorption, to experience more of Christ and less of self, we sometimes allow ourselves to spiral downward and become a victim of it.

We can learn to embrace the presence of suffering as fully and as joyfully as we welcome and embrace the absence of it. In fact, we are not truly free in Christ until we welcome sharing in His suffering as fully as we welcome sharing in the power of His Resurrection. And only the Holy Spirit can accomplish this miracle in our feeble hearts. Sooner or later we all must come to the place where we hear the Savior's voice deep with unfathomable pain calling us to the fellowship of suffering. And there we find His perfect, precious will folding us so closely we are wholly lost in Him. We find more of Him and less of us, and in that finding is unspeakable joy!

While words cannot adequately express the indescribable phenomenon of being loved by our God Who disciplines toward growth, the person who suffers with Him experiences the privilege and joy of that phenomenon in the deepest recesses of his/her heart. To be under the tutelage of the tests and trials of Our God Who Disciplines is indeed a privilege of the highest order. Thank You, Lord!

Daniel meets new born sister Joy Ann

Daniel plays with Joy Ann

"My soul, wait thou only on God,
for my expectation is from Him." Ps. 62:5

CHAPTER 4

Expectations

For the next eight years, things went somewhat smoothly in the Stratman household. Up to that point, each heart check-up had proven benign and no problems surfaced. Daniel played T-ball and was highly athletic. He appeared to be a normal, very active child. No one would have guessed he had a heart problem.

Shortly after his eighth birthday, Daniel had a check-up that showed his heart valve had significantly closed again. He was in the middle of a baseball season. Unable to play soccer, basketball, or anything aerobic because of his heart limitations, he had a beautiful attitude that simply reasoned, "If I can't play soccer or football, I'll play baseball." While Daniel was pleasantly adaptable, he was also very competitive. He was strong-willed, and as Susan puts it, he "had a mouth that wouldn't quit. Raising him was a challenge!" He loved to learn, and at a very young age knew that he wanted to be a cardiologist. A friendly, outgoing little boy, he was also a natural athlete.

And he loved his baseball games! The doctor said he needed another surgery, and could do nothing to exert himself. He had to stop playing ball, during the middle of the season. It broke his little heart. "We took him to a game his team played," says Susan, "which he should have been playing in himself. He couldn't handle it. We had to leave the field. It wasn't good for Daniel to get upset. The doctors said his heart was so fragile that even walking too fast could kill him. He basically could do nothing but watch television and play video games. Our friend, Kevin Smith, purchased a Game Boy for Daniel."

"Surgery was scheduled two weeks later, in December. I worked hard, emotionally, physically and spiritually to get myself ready for Daniel's surgery. Many people prayed for us. There were several prayer vigils, and one whole evening had been set aside by family and friends to pray for Daniel the week before surgery. We were prepared, ready for the operation. But Daniel spiked a fever while they were preparing him for surgery. The doctor ordered a culture and determined he had the flu. They sent him home. That was very difficult for all of us. When my expectations are shattered, it's really hard for me to regroup. It felt like I was on a roller-coaster."

Two weeks later the Stratman family returned to the hospital. Daniel's open-heart surgery went very well. His heart had been formed with a bicuspid valve, instead of the usual tricuspid valve, and those two sections were fused shut. Once again, as had been true when he was five-days-old, Daniel's surgeon did not have to replace the valve. The surgeon was able to do a valvotomy, clipping the valve into three loose flaps that flopped open, allowing the blood to move back and forth between Daniel's heart and body, causing a swooshing heart murmur as it flowed.

However, complications emerged after surgery. "That's when the roller-coaster began in earnest," remembers Susan. "When Daniel was in intensive care, his blood gases were not good. The next day he suffered bladder spasms that caused horrendous pain, screaming pain for him. Over and over he begged me to pray for him. I remember standing in the elevator pleading with the Lord, crying out to Him on Daniel's behalf. We were constantly up and down, down and up emotionally. My heart just wrenched when Daniel said something to me he must have heard one of the nurses say. 'Mommy, a little eight-year-old boy shouldn't have to go through this!'"

The fourth day after surgery, as they prepared to return home, Susan noticed one of Daniel's pupils was larger than the other. The lab ran a battery of tests but couldn't figure out what was wrong. Susan asked the neurologist if the problem could be related to the arterial line they put in his neck. The doctors finally ascertained that when they put the line in, they nicked the wall of the artery. It affected Daniel's sympathetic nervous system, and that's why his pupils were unevenly dilated. The problem was considered insignificant, so Daniel was sent home. He developed severe migraines as a result of that nick in his arterial wall, which lasted for several years.

Upon his release from the hospital, Daniel was cleared to play all sports except football. His natural athletic ability flowered fully on the soccer field and he became an avid player. Baseball took a back seat to his new first love.

Our God Who Never Disappoints

"When my expectations are shattered, it's really hard for me to regroup. It felt like I was on a roller coaster."

Placing our hopes and expectations in persons or events is a high risk endeavor for all of us. Over and over we are disappointed, our hopes are dashed, our dreams deflate and die, our emotions bourgeon back and forth, down and up, much like Susan's did. And yet we continue to do so, again and again. It's a human penchant we seem unable to discard.

Our loving God, Who knows what's best for us, does His utmost to turn us away from that futile behavior. He knows it's hard on us and hard on our relationships. All relationships struggle and stagger at least in part due to unmet expectations. God tells us to stop trusting in man, to trust instead in Him with our whole heart. He counsels us to make Him alone the desire of our heart, for He alone knows what the future holds, can meet all our needs, fulfill all our expectations, and satisfy our every desire (Ps. 118:8, Prov. 3:5).

I believe it was George Mueller, a wonderful, godly man of the nineteenth century, who learned how to place his expectations in God alone. God used George to establish orphanages in England for ten-thousand of His needy little ones. When George had a need he expected to be met, he would take a piece of paper and make two columns on it. One column he labeled "Pros", the other column he labeled "Cons". Then he took his hope, his expectation, and wrote it across the top of the page. He proceeded to write both the pros and cons of getting and not getting what he needed and expected. When both columns had equal weight, he would lay that paper face down, place the expectation squarely on God, and wait on God alone to do whatever His perfect will dictated. George didn't take his needs to human beings.

He was never disappointed. He knew that whether the Pros or the Cons column was met, he would be at peace and content, because George's will had been surrendered to God's, and his expectations rested in God alone.

For example, if George's transmission in his car went out his list might have included the following:

New Transmission Needed

Pros	Cons
1) no more walking to meetings	1) no more trim waistline
2) no more getting soaked in rainstorms	2) less opportunity to discipline the flesh
3) easier, more frequent trips to the grocery	3) more opportunity to buy things I don't need
4) more time freed up	4) less careful planning for profitable use of my time
5) less money spent on re-soling shoes	5) more money spent on gas

Of course, George Mueller didn't have a car, but the process is clear.

When the Holy Spirit tells us to "Delight yourself in the Lord, and He will give you the desires of your heart" (Ps. 37:4), He isn't speaking of a cause-and-effect dynamic, or a Santa Claus Syndrome wherein He gives us the things we want as a reward for delighting in Him. The Holy Spirit is telling us that when we take the time and allow Him to develop the passion within us to delight ourselves in Him, we will discover that He IS the deepest desire of our heart. He IS the One who satisfies our every longing. He is the Source of the unquenched thirst and the insatiable hunger we experience in our deepest, stillest, most poignant moments. Those moments erupt from deep within the very core of our being, the central places of our personhood. They give birth to our desires and expectations.

The more we delight in Him, the paler every other desire becomes. We begin to understand that all beauty is a mere and minimal reflection of Him Who IS Beauty. All human love is a paltry and imperfect reflection of Him Who IS love. Earthly things do indeed grow strangely dim in the Light of Who He is, and we discover we can do without them. Unmet expectations lose their power to de-energize and upset us. We find ourselves on fewer and less extreme roller-coaster rides. We begin to understand Asaph's rhetorical question in Ps. 73:25, "Whom have I in heaven, but Thee? And there is none on earth I desire besides Thee." We discover that our God Who is our All-in-All indeed never does disappoint us. He is the only One in Whom we can securely place our expectations. We experience a sweeter and a deeper peace as we yield our will to His, secure in Our God Who Never Disappoints. Thank You, Lord!

Daniel — a baseball fan from early on!

"God has gone out in front of you to strike the Philistine army." I Chr. 14:15

CHAPTER 5

Overcoming Odds

Upon returning from a mental break Susan and I had taken, she sat quietly in the prayer room where we were interviewing. With eyes emanating the Light she carried within, she spoke quietly and serenely.

"There are a couple of things I want to share with you about Daniel. When he was two-years-old, my dad said something about him that I have never forgotten. He said, 'There's something different about Daniel, I can't exactly put my finger on it. But that little boy has got to be just about the most spiritually discerning child I have ever seen.'"

When Daniel was two-and-a-half, his sister Jayme, who was almost five, accepted Jesus as her Lord and Savior. Daniel wanted to know how he too could get to heaven. For three days, in his little boy language, he kept asking Susan, wanting to know "How do I be saved?" Finally, on the third day, Susan stopped putting him off and asked him if he really knew what it meant to be saved. Daniel did know. He knew God made him and loved him. He knew God wanted Daniel to be in heaven with Him forever. He knew that Jesus was God's Son Who died on the cross to pay the price Daniel would have had to pay for the things he did that were wrong. He knew Jesus was the only One Who could pay for Daniel's sins and allow Daniel to be in heaven with God when he died. He prayed with Susan and asked Jesus to save him. Susan remembers telling Daniel that the angels were rejoicing in heaven because he was now a child of God. Daniel's eyes teared up with his excitement.

At age four, Daniel again began asking about salvation. He wanted to be sure he was saved. Susan says Daniel memorized the relevant Scriptures, and told his little friends about the Lord.

Daniel now, at age twenty-two, says he remembers confirming his salvation at age four, but he does not remember asking to be saved at age two.

Daniel always loved to read. He taught himself to read before he went to kindergarten, and could read the Bible well. "Daniel loved books about people who overcame the odds. Somewhere around the age of eight he read Dave Dravecki's books, *Come Back* and *When You Can't Come Back.* He would get up in the morning complaining groggily because he was awake until four o'clock reading in his bed. He couldn't put that book down. He devoured Dennis Bird's book, *Rise Up and Walk*, about a young man who was paralyzed on the football field. He read any books he could get his hands on about men who overcame great odds. Shortly before the surgery that devastated him at age eleven, he heard about Christopher Reeve and searched out everything he could find about that man."

Mouth agape, I listened to Susan unfold Daniel's history, humbled by the workings of our gracious, compassionate God as He prepared the way for a spiritually discerning child to face the horrendous, gigantic challenges and overcome the odds that would confront him in his future. What a loving, tender God He is indeed!

Our God Who Goes Before

"He read any books he could get his hands on about men who overcame great odds."

God's preparation of Daniel's heart to face the great odds that would soon be raised up against him reminded me of a similar event in David's life in I Chronicles. God went out in front of David to prepare the way for his victory over the great odds represented by the mighty Philistine army. In I Chronicles 14:13-16, the Holy Spirit tells us:

"Once more the Philistines raided the valley; so David inquired of God again, and God answered him, 'Do not go straight up, but circle around them and attack them in front of the balsam trees. As soon as you hear the sound of marching in the top of the balsam trees, move out to battle, because that will mean God has gone out in front of you to strike the Philistine army.' So David did as God commanded him, and they struck down the Philistine army, all the way from Gibeon to Gezer."

God knows our frame; He remembers that we are dust. He knows that we are weak and needy. C. S. Lewis writes, "Our whole being is one vast need, crying out for Him Who can untie things that are now knotted together, and tie up things that are still dangling loose."[5]

We simply cannot live a joyful, victorious life without God. And so He goes before and makes a way for us. Many times we look back on our lives and recognize what we didn't see at that time - God graciously and carefully preparing us for what He alone knew lay ahead.

I recall speaking with a newly-bereaved widow whose husband God had taken home to heaven one month previously. Mary spoke with gentle softness in her voice, reflecting the reverence, awe, and gratitude she felt as she described the first month of her life without her husband.

"One of the things I was most concerned about was sleeping alone, not having Bill in the bed next to me as he had been for so very many years. I dreaded that. I used to cry at night before he died, hoping he would get well, telling him how much I needed him, dreading the thought of waking in the night, turning over, and finding him gone. But God prepared the way for me by giving me little baby steps to take, one at a time."

"I remember the night the hospice nurse came and asked Bill if he wanted a hospital bed brought into the house. He said he did. As the cancer advanced, it was getting very difficult for him to go up the steps to our bedroom each night. But I couldn't bear the thought of us not sleeping together. The hospice nurse asked

Bill when he wanted her to bring the bed. Bill said, 'Right now, tonight!' I said, 'Oh Bill, couldn't we wait just a little longer? I'm not ready yet to give up sleeping next to you.'"

"Bill just looked at me with tired, sad eyes and said, 'Mary, I've been longing for this bed so I don't have to try to get up those stairs anymore'"

"And so they brought the bed. I slept on the couch in the living room by Bill's bed for the next two nights. I slept poorly, kept waking up, and was exhausted. My son counseled me, 'Mom, you have to go upstairs to bed tonight and get a good night's rest. I'll sleep down here by dad and make sure he's okay.'

"And I did. I was so tired, worn out, too weary for it to be as awful as I thought it might be. And Bill was downstairs nearby. So it was that God graciously and gently got me through my first night alone in our bed. I have seen God do so many things that way, gently and carefully going before me preparing the way for me, taking me one tiny step at a time as I walk one day at a time. It's so hard. But I've never felt so close to God before, so cared-for, and so loved."

Our younger daughter has been diagnosed with learning disabilities, celiac disease, joint malformation (five surgeries, more to come), and will be tested for aspergers syndrome in the near future. Each diagnosis has been difficult.

But God had prepared the way for me, had gone before me. For years at the Joni and Friends Family Retreats I have observed parents of folks who had been diagnosed with numerous disabilities. I have watched those families return to the retreats year after year, dedicated to caring for and giving whatever was needed to meet the needs of their loved ones. They have inspired and encouraged me. I have seen them do it, and do it well. Our God Who Goes Before had prepared my heart as He had David's and Mary's and Daniel Stratman's. He will prepare your heart also, to face whatever challenges He knows lie ahead. Thank You, Lord.

"The Lord has done this, and it is marvelous in our eyes." Ps. 118:23

Chapter 6

Charisma

Susan continued, "Another thing my dad said to me when Daniel was very young has proven itself to be true in a most remarkable way. Dad mused, 'You know, Sue, there's something about Daniel that draws people to him.' Dad was right. We have observed that happening for many years."

When Daniel was three-years-old, he was chosen to be the poster child for the American Heart Association, and that choice was repeated for several consecutive years. As a result, Daniel met extraordinary, stimulating people and experienced many exciting opportunities.

When he was eight, God gave Daniel special favor with Dr. Mark Payne, his new cardiologist. Dr. Payne nominated him as the miracle child for Children's Miracle Network. The Stratmans became deeply involved with that organization. Daniel did a lot of traveling on behalf of the Network, representing them in multiple ways. On one such trip, Daniel was to accept a check from August Busch IV of Anheuser Busch Brewery. Mr. Busch was flying into St. Louis from Texas on his private jet, and Daniel was to meet him on the runway. When he stepped off the plane, Mr. Busch shook Daniel's hand and began a casual conversation with him. Daniel told Mr. Busch he was there to "meet a big-shot, but I'm not sure who he is, so I'm just waiting for him." Mr. Busch quipped, "Well, while you're waiting for the big-shot, would you ask your Mom if I can take you on a helicopter ride?"

Daniel's pictures are a wonderful momento of that delightful event, and Mr. Busch continues to correspond with him as well as send him gifts. Mr. Busch's secretary told the Stratmans that Mr. Busch has a blown-up picture in his office of Daniel on the helicopter with him. Reciprocally, Daniel's heart holds a special place for Mr. Busch as well, for whom he prays frequently.

"Daniel's life has touched more lives that mine ever could," says Susan. "I just marvel at the things Daniel has done and the people he's met. I want these people to see not only Daniel, but, more importantly, his incredible God. We were deeply saddened recently when Sam Temperato died. We didn't have an opportunity to talk to Sam or his wife about the Lord. He was the man who started Dairy Queen in St. Louis. Daniel was featured on the cover of a magazine with him. So he knew Daniel, but Daniel did not have a chance to talk with him about his God. This book will help us, especially Daniel, tell people about his God. That's what Daniel wants."

The Cardinal baseball players know Daniel. He was asked to appear on the field with Yadier Molina, and also invited to be on the field for Christian Family Day.

"We have a close friend, Jon Glock, who's the Dean at Emmaus Bible College. He's been friends with Daniel for about eight years, and calls him Barnabus, in reference to Paul's traveling companion in the Bible. Jon speaks at camps all over the country, and likes to take Daniel with him. Daniel is an encouragement to Dean Glock."

Apparently Daniel is an encouragement to many people. God has chosen to give Daniel favor in their eyes, and has telescoped Himself through Daniel's life. It's really not about Daniel, and Daniel knows that. It's about God. It always is.

Our God Who Gives Favor

"Daniel's life has touched more lives than mine ever could."

Daniel's grandpa was astutely observant and time-proven-right when he said there is "something" about Daniel that draws people to him. That "something" is God-in-him, our glory, and the Lifter of our heads (Ps. 3:3)!! That Hebrew word for glory - *kabad* - means weight, splendor, honor, rich, to cause to be heavy with, abounding with, promote. When we do not stifle God's glory in us, how can we not attract others to us and to Him?!

God reveals Himself as One Who is intimately involved in our lives, not One Who loves us from afar, who keeps a kingly distance or a royal, proprietary mein. He determined what years, in which century, and in exactly what place we would live (Acts 17:26). He did this - and created us - so that we would seek Him, find Him and have fellowship with Him (Acts 17:27). He has a broad plan and a specific purpose for our lives (Jer. 29:11, Eph. 2:10). And in order to accomplish all of that, He turns the hearts of men and women whichever way He wishes, as needed. He does not force (Josh. 30:11-20), but He does indeed turn and give favor.

Daniel Stratman's story has strong parallels with the Biblical Daniel. In Dan. 1:9 the Holy Spirit tells us that God brought Daniel into favor with the chief official in authority over Daniel. Likewise, in Acts 7:10 the Holy Spirit shows us God gave Joseph favor with Pharoah, who appointed Joseph governor over Egypt and all Pharoah's palace. All three young men - Daniel, Joseph, and Daniel Stratman - had in common a God Who Gives Favor as needed in order to fulfill His perfect plan for our lives! Thank you, God!

American Heart Association – poster perfect!

"I will repay you for the years
the locusts have eaten..." Joel 2:25

Chapter 7

Restoring The Years

After the second open-heart surgery at age eight, Daniel once again did very well physically, spiritually, emotionally, and academically. However, Susan says it was not so for her. "I was not doing well. I appeared fine on the outside, but inside I was a mess. Those were years of frustration, guilt, unrest, and paralyzing fears for me."

"I love children. I always have. We were home-schooling our children, so I was around lots of large families who had babies. I was in turmoil about not having another baby myself."

"After our fourth child, Jay and I had decided we were not going to have more children; now I wanted some. So I was grieving that loss. I was also feeling guilty for having decided to have my tubes tied, for not letting God decide how many children we would have. I knew they were a gift from Him. I came very close to having the tubal reversed, agonizing over that option. I prayed for a miracle pregnancy, and cried each month when it didn't happen."

"And I was learning to trust God more. For the next two years I looked into foster care for new-borns, and adoption. I heard about two little girls in Japan who needed heart surgery, and also needed a family. I began pursuing that even though Jay wasn't crazy about the idea. But all that came to a screeching halt when Daniel's heart valve went bad again at age eleven."

There was one dynamic this time that Susan reports as very different from that of previous times; Daniel himself was very frightened. The Stratmans expected more surgery, but not until puberty. Daniel knew the doctors could not do another valvotomy. His valve was shot, which meant valve replacement was necessary with cadaver, pig-skin, mechanical, or artificial valve.

The doctors really didn't want to do that, because those kinds of valves calcify in children. It was not a good scenario. Additionally, their favorite surgeon, Dr. Thomas Spray, who had performed the two previous surgeries, left St. Louis and moved to Philadelphia. The Stratmans considered going there for the surgery, but after prayer and discussion they opted to go with the previous surgeon's understudy, who had observed both of Daniel's valvotomies.

A "Ross Procedure" was scheduled for Dec. 5th, 1995, wherein Daniel's aortic valve would be discarded, his pulmonary valve transposed to that place, and a cadaver valve inserted where his pulmonary valve had been. There were concerns about whether or not Daniel's body would reject the cadaver valve. This procedure was much more complex than the previous two had been, and there were greater risks involved.

All of this took its toll on Daniel. More than the inherent complications and risks, as well as the loss of his trusted doctor, the severity and trauma of the pain involved in the previous surgery had left its mark on Daniel's tender soul. He remembered well how it felt to be intubated, to have a breathing tube down his throat and not be able to talk. And he remembered with trepidation how much it hurt to have the tubes pulled out of his chest, stomach, and bladder. The bladder spasms had left a searing memory. Daniel was emphatic and outspoken in his opinion regarding surgery, as well as forceful in his resistance. Susan found these words scratched into a wooden table of hers, signed and dated by her son, "I DO NOT WANT TO HAVE SURGERY!" Fear stalked his little heart.

But our awesome God is a redeeming God Who promises to restore the years the locust has eaten and turn all things to our good. Susan was now able to use her many years of an intimate acquaintanceship with fear to help her son overcome his. Though she continued the ferocious struggle with her own fears, she took Daniel to the Scripture verses God used to sustain her whenever she became fear-filled. "I showed him how to lean on those promises God gives to His people, promises in Heb. 13:5, Ps.

56:3, and Deut. 31:6. 'Be strong and courageous. Do not be afraid or terrified for the Lord your God goes with you. He will never leave you nor forsake you. Do not be afraid. Do not be discouraged.' We sang songs about casting our cares on Him and trusting in Him Who will never leave us or forsake us. Every time Daniel would start crying and pleading, 'I don't want to have surgery, Mommy, I'm so scared, I'm so scared,' we would sing those songs and say those verses."

"And we prayed a lot. Daniel had a little ritual he would follow. Before any nurse pricked him for a blood sample, or any time he had a shot, before anything happened, no matter who was in the room, Daniel would tell them, 'You can't do it until my mom prays with me.' So we would stop and pray, no matter what. That ritual began when he was a little guy, probably five-years-old or so, and was still important to him when he was eleven."

"We had a group of other people praying for us also, not only before surgery, but on that day in the hospital with us. While Daniel was in surgery we prayed, read Scripture, sang, and prayed some more. Children's Hospital had private waiting rooms for families where they could do what they needed to do without disturbing other families."

"One verse we really leaned on in Daniel's battle with fear was Is. 41:10 which says, 'Don't be afraid, for I am with you...I will strengthen you, I will help you...' I wrote that verse on 3x5 cards and put them in Daniel's hospital room and bathroom the night before surgery."

"One of Daniel's best friends, Kevin Pickering, had given him a stuffed puppy for his eleventh birthday. Daniel wanted that puppy to come into surgery with him and the doctors said it was okay. So I took one of those 3x5 cards with Deut. 31:6 and attached it to the little puppy's neck. I did that for Daniel, but later that morning I thought, 'I hope those operating room personnel see that verse on that puppy.' I knew it would bless them."

"Well, they must have seen it. When they wheeled Daniel out of those surgery doors after that ten-hour surgery, all bandaged and hooked up to ventilators, I saw that puppy in his arms with a bandaged chest just like Daniel's! I just cried! They were so kind to him. And they knew he was terrified about having the tubes removed, so they kept him asleep in intensive care until all the tubes were removed."

And that was God's plan for Daniel, the way God met the needs of His frightened, precious little boy. In the months ahead, God would continue to meet the on-going needs of this family, who never in their darkest imaginings could have dreamed how very monumental they would be.

Our God Who Restores

"Susan was now able to use
her many years of an
aquaintanceship with fear
to help her son overcome his."

God promises us in Joel 2:25 that He will restore to us the years the locusts have eaten, painful times that appear to be wasted and devoid of meaning. He is a redeeming, sovereign God Who takes anything and everything and draws good from it in our lives (Rom. 8:28).

I reverently recall a breath-taking story that was stunning in its revelation of these truths and of the depths of love exposed therein, both God's and man's. At a Moody Bible Institute *Founder's Week*, a missionary whose name I've long forgotten shared a segment of her life in a deeply primitive jungle area of the African continent. For fourteen years or so she labored with the indigenous peoples, bringing the love and truth of Jesus Christ to them. Her long-suffering perseverance in the face of much natural adversity and the initial resistance of the people eventually turned their hostility to respect, and finally, to mutual love between the "white woman" and the tribal people. They worked together side-by-side in the daytime and gathered in the evening to listen to her stories of God's love for them.

One night as she slept, she was awakened by a rude hand that roughly clamped her mouth shut as others dragged her from her bed and into the jungle. There she was raped by many native men, all of whom she knew and loved. Disheartened, defeated, and completely confused, she returned to America to recover. Questions assaulted her mind, doubt plagued her heart. How could God allow those men, whom she still loved as brothers, to so abuse her and betray her? What purpose could there possibly be in such emotional and physical violence? She questioned God and waited on His answer.

Six months into her recovery, she was asked to share with a small group of women at a local church, to tell her story as part of a women's Evening of Renewal. She did so. Before she began, she noticed one young woman in her early twenties sitting on the front row, devoid of all expression and motionless, staring blankly ahead of her. The young woman remained in that condition for most of the missionary's story, until she began to share about the rape. At that point the young woman locked her eyes on the missionary's face, sat on the edge of her chair, and focused with riveting intensity. Tears began streaming down her face, and when the missionary finished, the young lady ran to her and hugged her tightly, sobbing as she poured out her own story of a gang-rape followed by suicide attempts in recent weeks. The missionary knew with deepest certainty that God's Spirit was telling her, "This is the answer you've been waiting for."

Evil does not originate in God, nor does He cause it. But He is Sovereign Lord over everything, and while people have free will to choose evil over good, God's Sovereignty works it for good for those who love Him and are called according to His purpose. Jacob's son Joseph in Gen. 30-50 emphatically and beautifully points out that what man intends for evil is meant by God for good. Evil does not triumph over good.

The missionary mentored the young woman, God's grace healed them both, and the missionary returned to her beloved people in Africa to serve and love them for another twenty years. Her testimony during Founder's Week was shared in her retirement years as witness to Our God Who Restores. Susan's ministry to Daniel, pulling on lessons learned from fear-filled previous years while still in the midst of that tenacious struggle herself, is likewise testimony to Our God Who Restores. Thank You, Lord!

Daniel – future cardiac surgeon

Daniel reports for clean-up duty

"A cheerful heart is good medicine."
Prov. 17:22

CHAPTER 8

The Calm Before The Storm

Protected under a thick prayer covering and the design of his sovereign God, Daniel breezed through his third open-heart surgery and returned home in four days. He wrote thank-you notes to his cardiologist and his surgeon, continued to plan on being a cardiologist when he grew up, and soon returned with renewed vigor and great zeal to the soccer field.

For the next six months, until Daniel's hernia surgery in July, God blessed Daniel and his family with a large portion of just plain fun. Susan describes those months as "just so good, everything was just so good. It was fun! We had so much fun!" Daniel was the healthiest he'd ever been, cleared by his doctors to do whatever he wanted, including football, which Susan was "not about to let him play."

Susan was president of the local chapter of the American Heart Association, representing them in Branson where she spoke to hundreds of people about Daniel's story. Daniel was involved in many television appearances, and participating in a large telethon for Children's Miracle Network. The entire family went to Six Flags, were treated to a nice hotel, Daniel appeared on television, and they had FUN!

Daniel's fame spread as he made numerous appearances with high-profile commentators. Ted Koppel, president of the channel eleven television station, took a shine to Daniel. More and more people began to recognize him. Susan was the proud mom, loving every minute of the spotlight and the drama. She looks back now and comments, "All of that stuff, it really doesn't matter in the big scheme of things, but at that time I was really caught up in it and having a great time!"

Meanwhile God was deepening Susan's relationship with

Him and strengthening their walk together. In His forever faithful, patiently persistent, winsomely wooing way, He had led her into two powerful Bible Studies that elicited growth in both her spirit and her character relative to obedience and trust. She did some grueling work on her persistent fear issues, making a commitment to the Lord that she would teach other women what He taught her about dealing with fear. Susan remembers finishing the Bible Studies and thinking, "God's about to do something in my life." She thought she was finally getting a handle on both the fear issues and on waiting on the Lord.

In June, Daniel's hernia emerged.

Our God Who Laughs

"...everything was just so good.
It was fun! We had so much fun!"

Over and over in His Word God reveals Himself as One Who desires for His people the "good" and "fun" Susan speaks of in the Stratmans' life. Ps. 37:3 beautifully summarizes four of God's desires for us. "Trust in the Lord and do good. Dwell in the land and enjoy safe pasture." How precious, how priceless is God's unfailing love, His continual effort on our behalf! He desires our good, seeks our good, and earnestly calls us toward our good. He wants us to enjoy life. His provision is for our enjoyment!

In I Kin. 4:21 God shows us His desired provision for His people: they ate, drank and were merry. God was pleased with the manner in which they did so, without irresponsibility, without gluttony, without drunkenness, sharing with the needy and the foreigner. He gave them peace on all sides, safety, and provided for each person his own vine and fig tree.

Only when we lose sight of the Provider does the provision become a danger to us. God knows our hearts are prone to wander. He knows the provision often replaces the Provider in the heart of the recipient. Prosperity is much more difficult to handle than adversity. God cautions us in Deut. 8:10-20 to be careful to praise Him for the provision He has given. He reminds us it is He Who gives us the ability to produce wealth, and He Who created the land on which we erect our buildings, often with materials He has fashioned. He speaks plainly, "Be careful that you do not forget the Lord your God, saying 'My power and the strength of my hands have produced this wealth for me.'"

Based on the whole counsel of God's Self-Revelation, it is clear that relationship is God's heartbeat, His essence, His very core and center. Forgetting Him, distancing ourselves from Him, seems to be the one phenomenon He simply cannot bear. For lack of more apt or fitting words whereby to speak of the unspeakable, we might merely say - it breaks His Heart. Things, provision, laughter, wealth, and health, can foster our relationship with Him, or interfere with it.

It seems we are the only creatures God has made who have the capacity for laughter, who CAN laugh. God loves to hear His people laugh! He says so clearly, numerous times and in numerous ways. In Prov. 15:15 He tells us that we who have a merry heart have a continual feast! Prov. 17:22 says that merry hearts do us good like a medicine. Prov. 15:13 counsels that a merry heart makes a cheerful face. The Hebrew word merry - *samach* - means bright, blithe, gleesome, glad, joyful, full of rejoicing.

Daniel with John Schneider "Dukes of Hazzard"

Our God laughs! We are made in His image. If laughter is good for us, and every good and perfect thing comes from above, as James 1:17 says, then Our God Laughs and wants us to laugh with Him! Hallelujah! Thank You, Lord!

Children's Miracle Network Telethon

"Wait for the LORD...I say wait on the LORD." Ps. 27:14

CHAPTER 9

Unprepared

Daniel's pediatrician wanted to have the routine hernia surgery performed at a little hospital in Washington, Missouri. Susan called Dr. Payne, Daniel's cardiologist, and asked if they needed instead to have it done at Children's Hospital. Dr. Payne did prefer the surgery be performed at Children's, so that they could monitor Daniel. If any complications emerged, they knew Daniel's history and could take care of it immediately. Surgery was scheduled for late July. The Stratmans met with the surgeon at Children's Hospital. He introduced them to an anesthesiologist they did not know, and who did not know Daniel. At the time, this raised no concerns.

In fact, the entire surgery raised no concerns; from their perspective it was "no big deal." The doctors and nurses had encouraged the Stratmans with comments that compared it to "a piece of cake compared to heart surgery". When Susan told others who had been prayer warriors previously on Daniel's behalf, they also "made light" of the surgery.

Susan now sees the problem therein. She did not consciously think or say, "For this surgery, we don't need God. This surgery we can handle by ourselves," but she says she behaved that way. She asked no one for prayer, so there were no prayer vigils, no prayer chains, and no one at the hospital to intercede for Daniel during what was scheduled as out-patient surgery. She comments, "It was a very hard lesson to learn".

Normally, the Stratmans were a praying family, a family steeped in prayer. When Daniel was recovering from his second open-heart surgery at age eight, he awakened with a tube down his throat, so he could not talk to Susan. He was trying to tell Susan something, and became very frustrated because he couldn't make her understand him. Susan suggested he spell it with his fingers for her. He spelled "p", "r", "a", and she knew the "y" would come next. So she prayed right then in the intensive care room. That was typical behavior for their family.

Daniel was busy at that time researching select-soccer teams. They were his current dream, his pressing goal, his momentary passion. Daniel threw himself into soccer the same way he threw himself into most things. He was passionate about God, and passionate about others knowing his God. He was passionate about sports and he was passionate about academics. Daniel did most everything with gusto.

He found a select team that had try-outs the week he was scheduled to be at summer camp. He persuaded Susan to pick him up early from camp so he could be there for try-outs, which he "passed" with flying colors. The soccer coach was so enamored with Daniel and his skills, he suggested they move his surgery up from late July to early July so Daniel would not miss any practices. The Stratmans agreed, and on July 8, 1996, they called the hospital to re-schedule Daniel's surgery. The date was changed to July 10th. Susan now reflects back on what they "missed" seeing at that time. It did not occur to the Stratmans to check with Daniel's cardiologist relative to the new surgical date. Unknown to them, Dr. Payne was on vacation. It also did not occur to them to pray about the change in date, to seek the Lord's counsel. They did not "wait on the Lord", a dynamic God had recently been teaching Susan with much emphasis. Nor did they tell folks they had changed the date. Susan says, "So no one was there, except my friend, Cindy, whom I told Wednesday morning, immediately before surgery. Cindy lives nearby, so she came up to sit with us. No one else was there, and almost no one even knew we were there." The Stratmans were not surrounded by family and multiple friends, were not covered with a thick prayer blanket, nor even remotely prepared for the tragedy about to unfold in their lives.

Steve Estes says that suffering sandblasts our soul to the core[6]. It wrings from it every hidden vestige of independence and wrests from it every hidden corner of prideful arrogance. A.W. Tozier writes that he doubts that God can use a person greatly until He has hurt him deeply. The Stratmans were about to discover the soul-wrenching agony of those terrible yet gloriously transforming truths.

Our God Who Answers Prayer

"...there were no prayer vigils, no prayer chains,
and no one at the hospital to intercede for Daniel
during what was scheduled as out-patient surgery."

In Jas. 5:16 God assures us that the prayer of a righteous man is powerful and effective. 1 Thes. 5:17 directs us to pray without ceasing, the kind of deep interior prayer that goes on all the time in that place where our spirit is united with Christ's Spirit and we are One. It defines and directs us, shining through the eyes of our souls, radiating Christ's love to everyone in every situation we encounter.

John Gibson Paton was born in 1824 in Dumfries, Scotland. He describes his father as a man of prayer who would enter his prayer closet numerous times daily. His eleven children knew that the continual movement of his lips in silent prayer was the source of the "happy light as of a new-born smile that always was dawning on my father's face: it was a reflection from the Divine Presence, in the consciousness of which he lived."[7]

There are literally dozens of definitions of prayer covering numerous aspects of it, occasions for it, and purposes in it. A most helpful perspective involves viewing prayer as conversation with God at any time in any place, for any godly purpose. It generally includes both speaking and listening.

However we attempt to define it, prayer remains a mystery. It is referred to hundreds of times in God's Word, there are inexhaustible treatises on the subject, and probably only a miniscule percentage of human beings who have never tried it. Yet it remains a spiritual enigma, something of which we can capture only a glimpse, a hint, a taste. Conversation with the omniscient, omnipotent, totally-other God-of-the-universe tends to be that way.

In Ps. 62:8 God exhorts us to pour out our hearts to Him, for He is our refuge. Prayer takes us into a conscious awareness of our relationship with God as the One Who wants to share our lives with us, wants to hear the deepest cries of our hearts and walk with us in all the gladdest, saddest, and maddest moments of our human journey. He can't get enough of us. Pouring out our hearts to Him pleases Him, draws us closer to Him, and opens us to His comfort and His counsel, as evidenced in Ps.118:5, "In my anguish I cried to the Lord, and he answered..."

God's responses to prayer are multiple variations of "Yes", "No", and "Wait". We have no way of knowing ahead of time exactly how they will look or what they will be. We do know with certainty that they do indeed come, and that in their unique variation they will reflect the mystery and goodness of His character and His relationship with us. They will be reflective of Who He is and who we are together.

Would prayer have changed the course of surgery that tragic day for Daniel? It's doubtful, for then instead of a loving God Who has a perfect plan for good for each of our lives, we would have a capricious God Whose answers are ultimately in our control, not His. Would the Stratman family and everyone who prayed for Daniel have benefited from doing so? Absolutely! Conversation with the One Who created us for His pleasure, and is deeply devoted to us, never leaves us untouched for the better. With Our God Who Answers Prayer it cannot be otherwise. Thank You, Lord!

Daniel – a healthy, happy boy!

"Oh LORD, how many are my foes!
How many rise up against me!"
Ps. 3:1

CHAPTER 10

Really Bad

On Wednesday, July 10, 1996, Jay and Susan Stratman sat calmly in Children's Hospital, chatting amicably as they waited for the surgeon to report on the outcome of Daniel's hernia surgery. God's gracious compassion was evident as He slowly unfolded, in little bits and pieces over the next few days, the news that would have simply been unbearable had the Stratmans been asked to comprehend it all at once.

Shortly after Daniel's surgery began, the head of the cardiology department, with whom the Stratmans were well acquainted, came into the waiting room and told them Daniel had "coded". His heart had stopped on the operating table, and he had been resuscitated. Dr. Johnson (not his real name) said they weren't sure why Daniel's heart had stopped, and referenced the anesthesia as a possible reason. He said they were putting Daniel on the floor (not into intensive care), and would keep him on a telemetry machine for the next twenty-four to forty-eight hours to see if there might be an additional, underlying heart problem of which they were unaware.

Susan and Jay were not distressed. Susan praised God for leading them to have the surgery performed at Children's, where they knew Daniel's history, instead of in Washington as originally considered. The cardiologist reported they were going to close Daniel up, put him in recovery, and notify the Stratmans as soon as he awakened. After calling several people and asking them to pray "because they think there might be a little underlying heart problem," Susan continued chatting in the waiting room with her friend Cindy.

At one point it occurred suddenly to Susan that it had been

two hours since the previous report. She began to experience some concern. After two-and-a-half hours and with accelerating anxiety, Susan told Jay, "This just isn't right!" A cardiology nurse, who had been Daniel's nurse during previous surgeries, walked into the waiting room. Susan knew from the nurse's countenance - as well as her walk - that something was terribly wrong. Alarmed, she blurted out, "Jenny, (not her real name) is Daniel dead?!?" Visibly upset, Jenny reported that Daniel was not dead but there was indeed a serious problem. "We're not sure what happened, but Daniel wouldn't wake up, and when he did wake up, he was posturing." Susan didn't know what "posturing" meant, or what it implied. Jenny explained that Daniel's arms were turned inward, his fists clenched, and he was having seizures. Once again, Susan and Jay did not grasp the full import of such body behavior, which is characteristic of severe brain trauma and injury. They asked Jenny what it meant, and she responded that they "really didn't know. Sometimes patients recover, sometimes they are left with some brain issues, sometimes they can't see. We're taking him to intensive care." All of those possibilities were true for Daniel, but God's mercy held-at-bay the stark truth that was Daniel's reality.

"Eventually," Susan says, "they took us in to see Daniel. He had tubes everywhere. I remember the sinking feeling in the pit of my stomach as I thought, 'I promised you no tubes, Daniel, I told you there would be no tubes!' The head of the cardiology department took us into this little waiting room by the intensive care unit. He was a mess. He looked terrible, like Jenny did, like he might drop over or pass-out. He just sat there. Finally he spoke words I'll never forget. 'This is really bad. I don't know what to tell you, except that I'm very worried. Daniel's stats are terrible. He probably will not make it through the next forty-eight hours.' "

Our God Who Is Sovereign

"...he probably will not make it through
the next forty-eight hours."

Perceived through a horizontal, human, medical perspective, Daniel "should not" have lived. Perceived through a vertical, spiritual, Biblical perspective we see clearly the sovereignty of God's Word in Job 14:5, "Man's days are determined. You have decreed the number of his months, and set limits he cannot exceed." Ps. 139:16 also reveals explicitly that "All the days ordained for me were written in Your book before one of them came to be." In Ps. 104 God tells us that when He takes away the breath of His creatures, they die. In 2 Kings 20, King Hezekiah asked God to increase his life-span, and God did so. As Job so beautifully declares in Job 1:21, "The LORD giveth, and the LORD taketh away. Blessed be the Name of the LORD!". God is Sovereign, and the first and last words are always His!

God is also good; therefore the first and last words are loving words intended for and orchestrated toward our good (Ps. 119:68). Hudson Taylor knew that reality well, and experienced it to a degree that is both inspiring and incomprehensible. Serving as a missionary in China, he writes of the earthly loss of his wife and son to cholera in the ninth month of her pregnancy. "From my inmost self I delight in the knowledge that God does or deliberately permits all things and causes them to work together for good to those who love Him. Deep was my delight in the consciousness that His will was being done (in taking them home to heaven), and that will, which was utterly crushing me, was good, and wise, and best."[8]

Many of us fear the will of God. But it is only in the doing of His will that we find our truest fulfillment, as well as our deepest satisfaction. Adrian Rogers said that the will of God isn't something we HAVE to do, it's something we GET to do. God chooses for us the very thing we would choose for ourselves if we had all the pertinent information needed and the good sense required to choose it. It's the best choice for everyone involved. God's tender heart must often ache because we do not see and do not trust His choices for us as our highest good. Samuel Wesley, who lived in the eighteenth century, wrote that he despaired of nothing because he firmly believed the He Who is best will do what is best. And thus Samuel cast his cares on God, and left the whole matter with Him to Whom he had committed all his concerns, without exception and without reserve.

If we are afraid of the will of God, it's probably because we're afraid of Him. And the only reason we could possibly be afraid of our God - Whose very character is the essence of Love - is because we don't know Him. And if we don't know Him, we can decide to seek Him, and His promise to us is we will indeed find Him if we seek with the full passion of our hearts.

George Mueller writes in his diary about the sovereign will of God during the illness of his beloved wife of thirty-nine years. "Yes, my Father, the times of my darling wife are in Thy Hands. Thou will do the very best thing for her and for me, whether life or death. If it may be, raise up yet again my precious wife - Thou art able to do it, though she is so ill; but howsoever Thou dealest with me, only help me to continue to be perfectly satisfied with Thy holy will."[9] When God took Mary home to heaven, George writes, "As a husband, I feel more and more (loss) every day that I am without this pleasant, useful loving companion...I miss her in numberless ways and shall miss her yet more and more. But as a child of God, and as the servant of the Lord Jesus, I bow, I am satisfied with the will of my Heavenly Father, I seek by perfect submission to His holy will to glorify Him, I kiss continually the Hand that has thus afflicted me; but I also say, I shall meet her again, to spend a happy eternity with her."[10]

In Daniel's case, as in Hezekiah's, the perfect will of Our God Who Is Sovereign included many more years of life on earth for Daniel. Thank You, God!

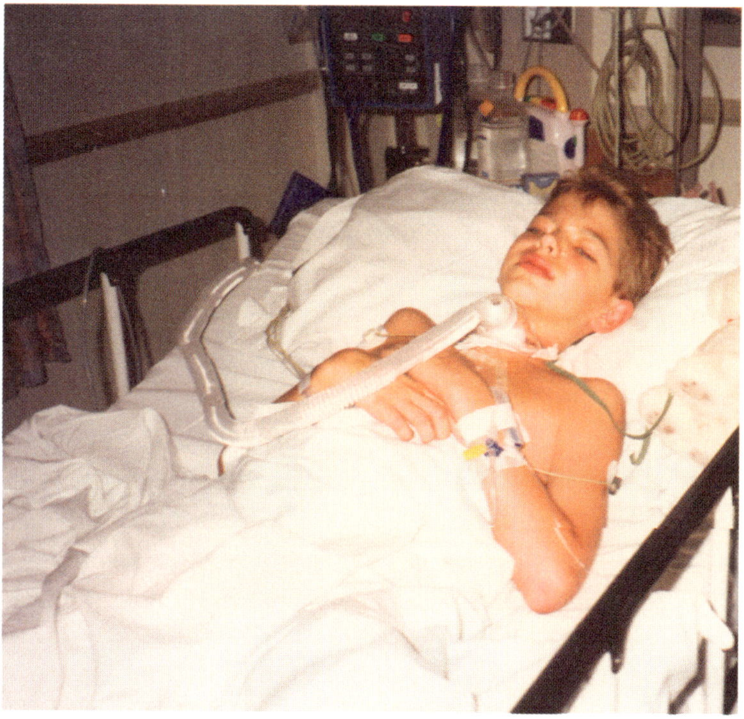

Daniel – fighting for his life

"Pray for us." Heb. 13:18

CHAPTER 11

Devastated

"To hear Dr. Johnson say that Daniel would probably not make it through the next forty-eight hours was terrifying," recalls Susan. "We were devastated. Everything crashed."

A merciful numbness quickly set in that allowed Susan and Jay to function, to begin making phone calls to solicit prayers and emotional support from family and friends. Because Jay is part of a non-denominational Bible church with branches throughout the U. S. and all over the world, within hours a mammoth network of prayers had been raised. Jay's brother flew in from Pennsylvania, and Susan's brother flew down from Wyoming. People converged from many places, so much so that it almost seemed to Susan as if a funeral were in progress.

It felt like a funeral as well. No one would give Susan and Jay information about what had happened in the operating room. Because no one would answer their questions, Susan and Jay, in that same ironic way that betrays children of divorce, began to feel guilty as if they, who were indeed innocent, had done something wrong. The entire hospital seemed caught-up in a pall of doom-and-gloom. A great number of medical personnel knew and loved Daniel from eleven years of frequent exposure to him. The administration knew him from appearances on television with Children's Miracle Network. The consistent message from hospital staff and the neurologist assigned to Daniel was that Daniel was brain damaged and would not live. Susan and Jay were encouraged to make a decision to turn off the multiple machines that were keeping him alive, and just "let him go".

But God had a different message for Susan and Jay. On Friday afternoon, two-and-a-half days after surgery, a physical therapist came into Daniel's room. She worked with him and talked with him, trying unsuccessfully to get him to move his muscles.

He was no longer having seizures or posturing. He lay without moving, hooked to a ventilator and tubes, eyes open, seemingly lifeless, with no apparent responses to anyone or anything. Susan watched the therapist's efforts.

"I thought I saw a muscle in his leg trying to move," reports Susan, "and I told the therapist. I said to Daniel, 'Daniel, remember Christopher Reeve!' Immediately tears began running down his cheeks. For the first time, I knew that he could hear and understand me. Naively, I told the therapist, 'He thinks he's paralyzed!'"

"I didn't know what I was talking about, of course. Daniel *was* paralyzed, but I was sure he wasn't because I knew he did not have a spinal cord injury, and I thought that was how people became paralyzed."

"Daniel was still crying - not moving, but crying. And I was also crying because I was so thankful that he understood what I said. I'm reassuring him he is not paralyzed, telling him that something happened in surgery but he's going to be okay. I told him he'd have to work hard and fight back just like Christopher Reeve did. My overwhelming experience at that moment was one of deepest gratitude. I couldn't wait to tell all those people who were praying for us."

That same Friday afternoon the anesthesiologist, Dr. Banning (not her real name), who had administered Daniel's anesthesia, once again came into Daniel's room to see him, as she had done previously on both Wednesday and Thursday. She was crying, as she had been on her other visits. She seemed to be in such turmoil, almost as devastated as Susan and Jay. She spoke to Susan and Jay with deep sincerity. "I don't know what happened. I just don't know what happened. If I made any mistakes, I'll never be able to work in the operating room again."

Susan remembers, "She actually made several trips a day down to Daniel's room to see him. She made no mention of a relationship with God. The Lord gave me such a wonderful opportunity to tell her about Jesus. For four weeks she was in and out of his room on numerous occasions."

Susan and Jay would later learn that not only had Dr. Banning been responsible for Daniel's brain injury, but she and a nurse anesthetist student also altered the records to exonerate her and make it appear that Daniel's heart was responsible for the injury.

Our God Who Turns All Things To Good

"The Lord gave me such a wonderful opportunity to tell her about Jesus."

Today, at age twenty-five, through an interpreter, Daniel says, "There is a Redeemer Who would love to love you because that is the one and only reason why He came to earth and put Himself on that cross - to save you and me from our sins and to save us from going to hell." Once that is accomplished, we can indeed spend eternity letting God love us.

Our God Who Turns All Things To Good immediately began His transforming work, using Daniel's tragic surgery for good. Since the time when Daniel was four years old, his heart's desire had been for other people to know about Jesus. However, his sphere of influence had been small, consisting of the few friends with whom he had shared his God. Suddenly Daniel's area of impact was greatly expanded. Without his awareness of it, his passion to share Jesus was being fulfilled. Not only was Dr. Banning impacted by the example and words of Susan and Jay, but the entire hospital staff recounted they had never seen anything like the outpouring of God's love through the Christian family and friends who rallied to the Stratman's side during the next few months.

Jay's family of Brethren Churches in the St. Louis area organized meals for almost a year for the Stratmans. Friends and cards came "by the truckloads", Susan says. The cards often contained money that people really couldn't afford to give. One family who visited the hospital weekly, knowing the limitations of Jay's public school teaching salary, put a hundred-dollar bill in Jay's hand each time they visited. Another friend of Jay's, who was also a teacher, took all of the Stratman's bills and paid them for several months. This particular friend had written Jay a letter the previous year on Father's Day informing Jay that it was God's love in and through Jay that had drawn him to want to learn about God and His Son Jesus. He and Jay taught school together, and God used Jay to show this friend Who He is and His great love for all of us. Susan and Jay do not know to this day how this friend paid all the Stratman's bills when the friend was supporting his own family on a teacher's salary.

While interviewing Jay, I asked him which characteristic of God has been etched most deeply into his heart in the eleven years since Daniel's injury. Without pause Jay answered, "His faithfulness, and the faithfulness of His people."

The hospital staff watched those faithful people come and go. They heard the conversations among them. They listened to their bedside prayers. They saw the love shining in the eyes of those visitors and Daniel's room covered in Bible verses. That love is the character quality of God that Daniel identified, in our interview, as the one that has been most deeply impressed upon his heart these past eleven years. The love in those visitors eyes was God's love shining through the eyes of His children. The hospital staff could not miss the joy that Jesus brings despite the circumstances that come our way. In fact, those circumstances become the platform on which we display our God. Hearts were softened, lives were changed, and our God Who Turns All Things To Good gave Daniel his heart's desire in a way he could not have anticipated. Thank You, God!

"My tears have been my food...
My soul is downcast within me."
Ps. 42:3a, 5c

CHAPTER 12

Cruel and Unfair

"On Tuesday night, one week after Daniel's hernia surgery, Dr. Payne came in to the hospital to see us," says Susan. "He was still on vacation, but nurse Jenny called him and told him what had been happening. He sat us down, and for the first time, the truth was laid-out before us. My heart recoiled in horror and my throat closed up with pain as he told us Daniel was severely brain injured, would not recover, and if he did survive at all, would be a vegetable. He also said he was demanding an investigation to find out exactly what happened in the operating room. I remember spitting out my pain, 'I don't care what happened, it doesn't matter to me, I just want my son back!' Dr. Payne was so wise and kind. He told me, 'But you WILL care, Sue, and you will need to know.'"

"Jay and I went downstairs where Larry, a pastor-friend, was waiting to take us to dinner. The thought of food was nauseating. We were totally undone. And my anger had begun to surface. I remember irrationally accosting Larry. 'There's no God! This is the work of satan. If God is going to let a little boy who survived three open heart surgeries live as a vegetable, there's just no God, and I'm done. I will never believe in Him again! This is CRUEL! This is unfair and cruel!!'"

God used Larry at that moment to speak words to Susan that both validated her anguish and strengthened her flailing faith, words she will never forget and cherishes still today. With the compassion of God's tender heart and the wisdom He gave Solomon, Larry blessed Susan. "Sue, right now your emotions are stronger than your faith, but your faith will recover." Our gracious God knows it takes time and much heart-searching for anger to be overcome by trust and anguish to give way to peace.

God does not abandon us, nor turn His back on us, nor retreat to a sanctimonious distance when we are undone. He draws even closer, He comforts our ravaged hearts through the care of others, and saves His choicest cordials for our deepest devastation. Mrs. Charles Cowman in Streams In The Desert describes a cordial as one of God's choicest blessings chosen by Him for us at a time when we are at the end of ourselves, have no hope of carrying on in life, and desperately need a heart-lift. Susan was to receive one of those cordials the next afternoon as she wrestled and grappled with her newly-grasped, intensely-unwelcome reality.

Outside Children's Hospital Susan paced, back and forth, round and round in a circular pattern, treading the same path over and over again, seeking, needing, pleading for relief from her agitated anguish, desperate for answers. Roaring and shifting like a giant earthquake splitting the ground beneath her, it was shaking her senseless.

"Why, Lord, why would You do this to us? Daniel is an athlete, he excels in sports, he's an eleven-year-old child and our only son! How dare You, how could You let this happen to us?" With an unholy boldness breaking out from the depths of her destitute soul, Susan dared to question and even challenge her Sovereign Lord.

"In the very same path I had been pacing for the last ninety minutes lay a tiny sparrow on the ground, dead, where it had not lain before. I looked at it, surprised to see it there within my well-trod sphere. And finally, wonderfully, faithfully, God broke through to my broken heart. I heard Him clearly, in my spirit, reassuring me, comforting me, reminding me that if He cares for the sparrow and not one of them falls to the ground apart from His will, then surely He is adequate and able to care for Daniel, to care for me and for our family. He would make a way where there seems to be no way." More wrestling, more grappling with herself and with her God lay ahead both for Susan and for Jay, but God's promise through the sparrow to care for Susan and her family remained with Susan throughout the years, encouraging her and comforting her.

One such time of wrestling occurred two-and-a-half-weeks later as Daniel remained motionless, without any movement, silent and unresponsive to the overtures of his family, friends, and physical therapist. One evening, without preamble, he began exhibiting an extreme agitation that manifested with his heart rate accelerating to two-hundred-plus beats per minute, a fever of one-hundred-five degrees and the sweat of a marathon runner. Tears streamed down his face, he cried and cried, unable to make any sound whatsoever. He had a trache tube in his throat to help him breathe and a feeding tube in his stomach. He needed continual changes of clothing and bedding. The agitation continued around-the-clock, lasting interminably. Daniel did not sleep, Susan and Jay did not sleep, and, as Susan so aptly describes it, "We were all just a mess". The doctors kept changing medication, explaining that Daniel's brain was working overtime in an attempt to organize and make sense of the shambles of his body system.

Susan marvels at the way God strengthened them during those grueling days and nights. When Jay fell apart, God kept Susan strong. When Susan fell apart, God gave Jay strength. And so they experienced and lived the beautiful truth of Eccl. 4:9a,10, "Two are better than one...if one falls down, his friend can help him up." They also experienced the precious truth of Matt. 12:20. Susan and Jay were bruised reeds and smoldering wicks that our God took great care to keep from being emotionally and spiritually broken and snuffed-out.

Later, Susan would remember the truths she had believed for many years, but whose reality had been blunted by the hammering of recent blows. If God were "fair", we would all be headed for hell, Jesus would never have lived, died, or been raised from the dead, our sins would be unforgiven, and there would be an irreversible gap between God and us. Our relationship with Him would be one of hostility, and our enmity would mean eternal, spiritual death for us. For all of us have sinned, and fall short of the glory of our gracious, forgiving God.

Our God of Choicest Cordials

"He would make a way where there
seems to be no way."

It has been ever thus. God always intervenes and makes a way when His beloved children are overwhelmed. He promises us He will do so in I Cor. 10:13 wherein He states, "No temptation has seized you except what is common to man. And God is faithful; He will not let you be tempted beyond what you can bear. But when you are tempted, He will also provide a way out so that you can stand up under it."

God's Word reveals His history of intervening when His beloved children are overwhelmed, and that allows us to place our deepest and most desperately needed trust in Him. History is riddled with His choicest cordials being lavished in our direst needs. We all experience those needs, and if we have eyes to see, we all are granted His choicest cordials.

Elijah is a suitable example. God had shown Himself strong again and again in Elijah's history, in most astonishing ways, and yet, like Susan's, Elijah's emotions momentarily overruled his feeble, flagging faith (I Kings 19:1-9).

God looks at our hearts. He refuses to let the momentary impatience of our angry grief trump the eternal patience of His everlasting love. He cares about His relationship with us so much more than He is concerned with isolated, uncharacteristic behaviors that erupt in times of darkest stress. His honor is not diminished by our dishonor. He is so much more compassionate than we are. Our hearts are far more condemning and critical than His heart is. Our victories bring far more delight to Him than our sins and defeats bring disappointment. God had complete foreknowledge when He created us, He knew our hearts were prone to wander, and our failures and flaggings do not surprise

Him. He created us for His pleasure, in His likeness, and He delights in who we are. He hates our sin, yet He loves us deeply.

And so as Elijah sat down on the job, under the broom tree, filled with fear, depressed, and praying that God would let him die, God gave him rest for his weary soul. Elijah fell asleep. In time, God sent an angel to waken him, and provided food and water, after which He again gave Elijah rest. Some of the most encouraging, comforting words in all of God's Revelation were then spoken to this discouraged, devastated man. Accompanied by the reassuring strength of a soothing touch, the angel spoke words that eliminated any lingering doubts that might have remained in Elijah's troubled heart about the understanding compassion of his all-powerful God. "Get up and eat, for the journey is too much for you."

And so it is. Our journeys oftentimes do indeed prove to be too much for us. Susan and Jay's journey had become unbearable. Without God's intervention, they would not have managed. With God's intervention they and we not only manage, but emerge from our battles victorious, for God always works in us to will and to do of His good pleasure (Phil. 2:13). Few things give Him greater pleasure than to see us take Exodus 14:14, 13 seriously. "I will fight for you. You need only to be still. Stand still, and see the salvation of the Lord, which He will accomplish for you today." He causes us to stand firm in Christ and leads us in victorious procession throughout our journey. He lifts us out of the miry clay and horrible pits into which we climb or in which we find ourselves. He stands us on solid ground and puts a new song in our hearts that banishes depression and discouragement, which is exactly what He did for Job.

Job found himself in a horrible pit of miry clay through no fault of his own, according to God's Word. Job was a godly man, the greatest man in the East, and one whom God describes as having four highly notable characteristics: perfect, upright, fearing God, shunning evil. The Hebrew word for perfect - *tam* - means complete, morally pious, gentle, dear, undefiled. The Hebrew word for upright is synonymous with "just". And yet

Job was a paradox-of-a-man, as we all are, a man who committed sin. The whole counsel of God's Word makes it emphatically clear that there is only One Man Who never sinned, and His Name is Jesus. We humans have a penchant for creating heroes, and oftentimes Job is presented as a hero in Bible studies. But Job is not a hero; there is only one Hero, and His Name is Jesus. Job is actually not even a consistent role-model. Except for Jesus, there are no consistent role models in Scripture, only mirrors that reflect both our saintliness and our sinfulness.

After initially responding admirably at the loss of family, possessions, and health, depression grips Job like a vise, and holds him tightly in its grasp until God releases him near the end of his journey. Job does not curse his God, but he curses the day of his own birth, longs for death that does not come, and admits to bitterness of soul (Job 3:20-21); Job was a worrier (1:5, and 3:25,26), boldly speaks out of the bitterness of his soul, and rails against God (7:12-21), in the midst of a pity party. He becomes deeply confused about God's character (9:21-35), and his too-small perception of our very-big God does not serve him well. His diatribe against God imputes God with evil intent (10:1-22). In short, Job is totally undone, or, as Susan would say, "a mess!!" My heart aches for him in 10:20 wherein he asks his God to turn away from him and leave him alone so he can have a little comfort in his last few days of life. Alas - apart from God, there is no lasting comfort.

But while God's heart most assuredly aches with His dear Job, God isn't put-off or even angry with him. He knows Job's heart and Job's deep love for and fear of Him. He knows Job speaks from the depths of his depression pit as he reels from the pummeling of his well-intentioned but bumbling, blathering friends. (I've done a bit of bumbling and blathering myself on occasion, more frequent than I care to mention.) God is not pleased with Job's response to suffering (38:2, 18,) and does challenge him about contending with God (40:1-8). God wants Job to grow in his relationship with Him. God knows our faith isn't reliable until it's tested.

In chapters 38 through 41 God fulfills the desire of Job's heart that Job has spoken of in 19:25-27 and 23:3. Job yearns to see his God with his very own eyes, himself, not as others have seen Him but as God would show Himself uniquely and personally to Job. God now grants him the desire of his heart: Job's eyes see Him in the incredibly awesome and detailed description of Himself God lays out for His dear Job (39 and 40). Our God Of Choicest Cordials gives Job the cordial He had been reserving for this very time, just as He did for Susan, and just as He will do for you and me. Thank You, Lord!

So very loved!

"For I know the plans I have for you," declares the LORD, "plans to prosper you and not to harm you, plans to give you hope and a future."
Jer. 29:11

Chapter 13

Amazing Grace

For four weeks after Daniel's surgery, the anesthesiologist, Dr. Banning, was a continual presence in the Stratman's lives. Both in Daniel's room and in the waiting room outside the intensive care unit where Susan and Jay went for breaks in the long, intense days of waiting, Dr. Banning would come and sit with them. Often she would cry; sometimes she would share her troubles with them. Her mother had recently died of cancer, her father was suicidal, and her husband was dying of a lung disease. Susan and Jay grew to care for her, and through them, God's love enveloped her, though Dr. Banning did not recognize or understand its Source.

Two days after Daniel's hernia surgery, Dr. Banning had, amidst weeping, and with deep sincerity, declared that if she had made any mistakes that caused Daniel's brain injury she would never again be able to work in the operating room. "It was amazing," posits Susan, "that God gave me this incredible strength to share with her my relationship with Him. I told her, 'Don't blame yourself for this, God has a plan for my son's life, and for some reason, even though we cannot understand it, His plan involves this. All of this is part of God's plan for Daniel's life.' Dr. Banning seemed to have no grasp of what I was saying. She made no apparent response."

"When Daniel was finally moved from intensive care to a regular hospital room, he had a roommate with a baby who cried continually. It was very difficult for us. Dr. Banning went to the powers-that-be and arranged for us to move to a private room, which was such a blessing to us!"

"Toward the end of the fourth week, on Thursday morning, I took Dr. Banning a basket I had prepared for her. I didn't know that the very next day, Friday morning, we would discover from the investigation results that it was she who had made numerous errors - and then altered the records - that resulted in Daniel's brain injury. The basket had lots of goodies in it, lots of stuff, including a Bible, a Daily Bread devotional, and tracts explaining how much God loved her and wanted a relationship with her. I gave the basket to her."

"That same morning Dr. Banning told us that she had been asked to leave us alone, not to see us anymore, and that she would probably lose her job. She said there was going to be a press conference the next day, as a result of the investigation that Dr. Payne had ordered. I so clearly remember standing in the kitchenette outside the little nurses area and hugging Dr. Banning, crying with her, and praying with her. The Lord gave me such a tender heart toward her because she was hurting so bad. I felt so sorry for her."

"The next morning, on Friday, August 9th, after four weeks of intense and difficult waiting, weeks of trying to make sense out of apparent craziness, with Daniel fighting for his life, with Jay and me trying to decide whether or not to turn off the machines keeping Daniel alive, we finally learned from Dr. Payne and the head of anesthesiology exactly what had happened in the operating room during Daniel's hernia surgery. That's when, in retrospect, we realize we fully experienced God's grace in amazing ways."

Our God Of Higher Ways

"Don't blame yourself for this,
God has a plan for my son's life."

With astonishing certainty and a stellar faith that had recovered well from previous faltering, Susan asserted that God had a plan for Daniel's life, a truth she had known and experienced for many years and in many ways in her own life. With the incredible, supernatural power of amazing grace she reached beyond her own devastating confusion and laid hold, by faith, of the path wherein mountains and valleys become plains. Choosing NOT to walk by sight, she comforted and encouraged a woman whose walk <u>was</u> limited by sight.

God's ways are not our ways, and His thoughts are not our thoughts. Of this, He assures us with great contrast in Is. 55:8,9. "As the heavens are higher than the earth, so are My ways higher than your ways, and My thoughts than your thoughts." Oftentimes, we forget that this is so. We need to learn to interpret our circumstances by the goodness of God, not interpret God's goodness by our circumstances.

Corrie Ten Boom struggled with bitterness and hate as she and her sister Betsy experienced the agony of the concentration camp at Ravensbruck. Betsy continually exhorted Corrie with reminders that she could not hate others and still have a close, intimate relationship with Jesus. Corrie forgot God had a plan for her life. Betsy remembered. She assured Corrie frequently that, when God's timing was right, and they were released from Ravensbruck, they would travel the world telling others that there is no pit of despair so deep God is not deeper still. And, she declared emphatically, the world would believe them because they had experienced the pit of Ravensbruck. It proved to be so. Corrie spent thirty years after her release watching God use her testimony to unfold His plan as she traveled in sixty countries bringing new believers to Himself, and deepening His relationship with former friends of His. And though God had taken Betsy home to heaven while she was still in Ravensbruck, her precious presence and her sterling testimony did indeed travel the world as Corrie told Betsy's story along with her own.

Oftentimes God's plan is so incredibly higher than ours in its vast generosity and wild extravagance that we simply cannot comprehend it. Our capacity is limited; no container can hold more than its capacity. His lavish extravagance, however limited our comprehension, does grant us a foretaste of heaven, wherein eye has not seen, ear has not heard, and our hearts have not begun to imagine the beauty and wonder and glory and joy God has prepared for us simply because He loves us! In the face of such lavish love we feel as if we might somehow implode, combust into an inner flame, a veritable fire, a thousand hosannas accompanied by a zillion fireworks, as Father Tim experiences in Jan Karon's Mitford Series. Sometimes our hearts swell up with so much love for God it closes up our throats with pain. Such was the case for James Warnock and his dear young family.

Recently my husband and I attended the Andy Williams Christmas Concert in Branson, Missouri. The John Norton (name changed) family performed with Mr. Williams, and after the concert, allowed me to interview them at their sales table. With a smile in his voice, John is quick to testify to the reality that God's plans are higher than ours, and are plans for good, to give us hope and a future. John, father of five lovely, talented daughters - all of whom love Jesus - spent summers traveling with his family on the state fair circuit, performing vocal concerts wherever a venue was available to them. With a deep love for music and no money for professional lessons, his daughters were home-taught. Folks who heard the family sing frequently told them they should move to Branson, Missouri, a mecca for family-oriented performers.

One summer they finished their fair circuit with ten days remaining before school began in the fall. So John took his family to explore the Branson about which he had heard so much. He liked what he saw, and asked God to show him if and when his family should consider moving there. After two years of family prayer and preparation, John deemed his young family ready, and they risked the move to Branson. His daughters ranged in age from fifteen down to seven.

Within one year of their arrival their entire savings account was gone, bilked by unscrupulous theatre owners and folks who took advantage of the naivete of newcomers. Anxious and uncertain of their future, God rescued them via a seasoned performer who teamed up with them for two years before he closed his show. Without money and without a means of financial support for his family, John prayed frequently for God to open doors and reveal His plan for them. One evening he took their Christmas CD to the office of the Andy Williams "Moon River Theatre", one of hundreds of people who have made a similar effort throughout the years. The next day Andy Williams listened to the CD, called John, and invited the astonished family for an audition. Pleased with what he saw and heard, Mr. Williams invited them to do a preshow for his concerts. The following year they were promoted to a full-time place in Andy Williams' Christmas Concert. Our God Of Higher Ways alone has power to open such doors in the face of incredible odds, for the Nortons, for the Stratmans, for you and for me, to do what He plans for us to do in His Jer. 29:11 promise! Thank You, Lord!

"Though the mountains be shaken, and the hills be removed, yet My unfailing love for you will not be shaken..."
Is. 54:10

Chapter 14

He's Still God

"On Friday morning," Susan remembers, "we were told that Dr. Banning had failed to set a blood pressure reading during surgery, had set the anesthetic machine too high and for too long, then left the room, leaving Daniel with a nurse anesthetist student who was there only to observe. Dr. Banning went to another operating room to start another child's surgery, then went to the bathroom, where she was paged when Daniel coded." (In 1996 it was acceptable at this hospital for an anesthesiologist to leave one operating room to begin another surgery in another room. The Stratman's tragedy became the catalyst for a change in that policy.)

The blood pressure cuff, had it been set properly, would have monitored Daniel's blood pressure every two-to-three minutes. Eleven minutes into surgery, the surgeon noticed something didn't "look right," although Susan can't remember if it was the blood flow, the blood color, or the organ color. The surgeon asked the student anesthetist, "Is Daniel okay?" The student answered "Yes." Then he looked at the blood pressure monitor and noticed the number had not changed in eleven minutes. He hit the reset button and instantly Daniel's blood pressure was 34 over 13. He hit it again, and it was still lower. He knew something was terribly wrong. Daniel's heart stopped immediately after that. They called code, administered epinephrine, did compression, got his heart going, but the damage had already been done to his brain.

Susan and Jay were devastated anew. Jumbled emotions, racing thoughts, anger, despair, and a sadness that penetrated bone and marrow laid hold of their souls. Error. Human error had caused the loss of so much that was so very precious to them, error that could have been prevented, that seemed so totally unnecessary, so vastly incomprehensible, so senseless and so hopeless.

Concern for Daniel kept the Stratmans from sinking into the yawning abyss of despair that seemed to hover near the edges of their souls. "Daniel was still not stable," Susan says. "The head neurologist was continually trying to prepare us for Daniel's death. His heart rate remained over 200, and Dr. Keith (not his real name) was sure Daniel's heart would give out. He told us to take Daniel home and change his diapers and try to get on with our lives. He seemed so stoic, so cold and hard with no emotion whatsoever. Whenever I would mention an improvement I observed in Daniel, such as a toe moving, he would say 'No, you didn't see that, there is nothing there,' I really didn't like him."

"But that all changed one day when God showed us the terrible pain and struggle going on inside this man's heart. He came to us one afternoon and told us he was removing himself from our case. 'I'm taking a three week leave, and turning you over to Dr. Sinclair (not his real name). He's a wonderful neurologist; he'll take very good care of Daniel.' Then he walked out of the room, turned around, and came right back in with tears in his eyes. He blurted, 'I don't know how you're doing this. I go home and I think about Daniel, I see my little boy and I think about Daniel, and I'm at the hospital and I can't get my mind off Daniel. I don't understand how you people are handling this as well as you are.' And he walked, crying, out of the room."

"When I stop now and reflect on all God was doing during those four weeks, I am just amazed. He was still God, He never changed. We went back and forth, up and down, shaken or steady, but God never changed. He remained as strong and as faithful as He had ever been. He was still God, and that kept us sane."

Our God Who Is Faithful

"...God never changed. He remained as
strong and as faithful as He had ever been.
He was still God..."

God knows what bitterness and unforgiveness do to our hearts, our bodies, and our souls. We were not designed by our Creator to carry bitterness. It poisons the container far more than the one toward whom it is directed. Medical science has long recognized the physical damage done by an unforgiving heart. And God has warned us repeatedly about the havoc it inflicts in our lives. God likens it to a contaminating root that spreads its multiple feelers outward and causes trouble, defiling everyone within its reach.

Bitterness settles into our souls over a period of time as we develop a way of thinking about a person that is contrary to God's will. It becomes a stronghold within us wherein we give satan legal jurisdiction and upon which he can pitch his tent and torment us with fear, anger, worry, depression, and other destructive emotions. Each time we allow the sun to set on our anger we strengthen satan's hold on that corner of our hearts, giving him more ground upon which to operate. "Do not let the sun go down while you are still angry, and do not give the devil a foothold (place, location, home, license, stronghold, an area of legal control)" Eph. 4:26,27. Angry thoughts and feelings that are not checked mushroom into hate. A tender, touching exchange relative to the tragedy of embittered hearts occurs in a conversation between Father Tim and Nurse Kennedy in Jan Karon's novel These High, Green Hills.

"There's something I've been wanting to ask you, Father," said Nurse Kennedy, walking with him along the hall.
"Shoot."
"Why is it God so often breaks our hearts?"
"Well. Sometimes He does it to increase our faith. That's the way He stretches us. But there's another reason, I think, why our hearts get broken."
She looked at him.
"Usually," he said, "what breaks is what's brittle."
She nodded thoughtfully. "So we have to be careful of getting hard-hearted?"
"Bingo," he said, putting his arm around her shoulders as they walked to the end of the hall.[11]

We guard against hard, embittered hearts by making a firm decision, with God's grace, to stand ready always to give up, turn loose, let go of everything we have. It has all been given by Him, for every good and perfect gift comes from above. When, in His perfect time and will, He takes back what He has given, we can find strength to let go of the gift by clinging to the Giver.

Susan and Jay, as well as their entire family, were deeply vulnerable at this time to roots of bitterness springing up in their lives. The natural, fleshly thoughts Susan and Jay experienced relative to Dr. Banning would have, over time, developed into a way of thinking about her that would have been contrary to God's will. "She should not have left the operating room. She should not have made the errors. She should be perfect. She should have performed flawlessly. It's all her fault. She should be stripped of her license. She has ruined Daniel's life and our lives." Such thought patterns would gradually but definitively harden their hearts, eroding their peace and their capacity for joy. Consequently, God faithfully and carefully arranged specific timing in which to reveal specific insights that would allow their hearts to remain pliable, to soften with compassion and forgiveness rather than harden into resentment and bitterness.

Weeks before Susan and Jay knew with certainty that Dr. Banning's errors were responsible for Daniel's injury, He gave her favor in their eyes and warmed their hearts toward her. The hours Dr. Banning spent weeping over Daniel, the angst she had shown relative to her responsibility, relative to his injury, - even though she failed to fully admit it and did indeed alter records to hide it - and the sharing of her own personal problems, made her a real human being in their eyes, a flesh and blood person experiencing her own difficulties, vulnerable to pain just like we all are. She had a face, a presence, a heart. Their immense gratitude toward her for previously arranging relief and respite from a frequently crying baby on a daily basis placed them in a posture of receptivity as opposed to one of rejection and revenge.

God had made a way for compassionate, merciful thoughts toward Dr. Banning that promoted forgiveness and protected against bitterness. "Dr. Banning is human. She made errors, yes, but not on purpose. She can't be perfect, none of us can be perfect. She feels terrible about it. She was afraid of losing her job, that's why she altered the records. I'd be afraid, too, if I were going to lose my job. I make mistakes in my teaching, but my mistakes don't cost as much as hers do. It must be awful to know you can kill someone by making a mistake in your work. What terrible pressure that must be. And she's been under terrible pressure at home also, in her personal life. She didn't do this on purpose. It was an accident. If I cause an accident and kill someone with my car, I want the family to forgive me, not hate me. Please help me forgive her, God. Please don't let me become bitter."

Hebrews 12:15 makes it clear that God's grace alone gives us the supernatural power to forgive offenses and wounds we have received, avoiding the bitterness that unforgiveness brings. During our entire three days of interviewing I saw no hint whatsoever of unforgiveness in Susan, Jay or Daniel's hearts, an astonishing fact indeed.

Unforgiveness, bitterness, and resentment rob us of our

intimacy with God. As long as we separate ourselves in unforgiveness and bitterness from even one person, we distance ourselves from God, in Whose image they are made and of Whose breath of life they partake.

No human being other than ourselves can rob us of our joy and our peace. They come from God. But loss of our peace and joy, as well as our health and spontaneity, is the price we pay when we choose bitterness. Our God Who Is Faithful knew Jay and Susan could not bear that additional burden. He protected them, as He will you and me if we allow Him. Thank You, Lord!

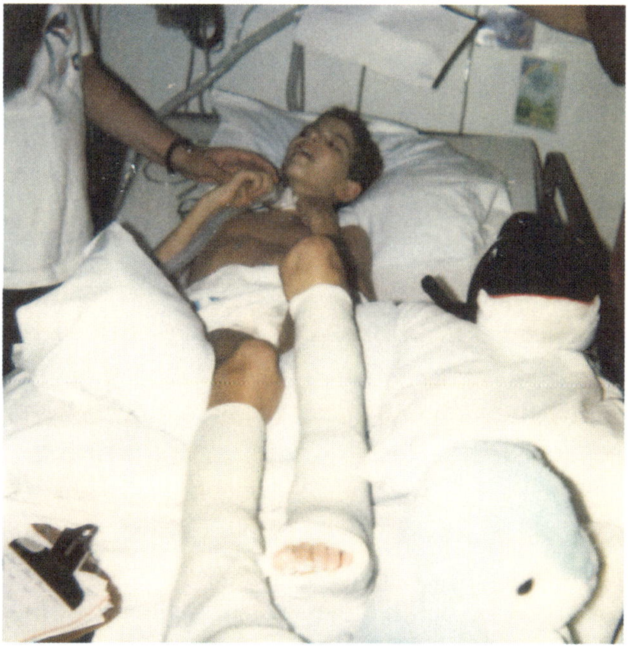

Casts to fight the fetal posturing

"Why are you downcast, o my soul?
Why so disturbed within me?"
Ps. 42:5

Chapter 15

Miry Clay and Horrible Pits

Although God's grace prepared Jay and Susan to reject the roots of bitterness and unforgiveness relative to Dr. Banning and Dr. Keith, there remained a marathon emotional and spiritual battle with anger and grief that challenged them for the next three months.

"Jay was fairly steady through all of it," says Susan. "When he did get angry, he got angry with Dr. Banning. When I got mad, I got mad at God. Whenever I would reach a breaking point, God would send exactly what I needed, at just the right time," says Susan. "Both the battle and the way God walked me through it were incredible."

"I was especially vulnerable every month right before my menstrual period. I just crashed. I would get really, really, really angry with God. I remember one time Daniel was still in intensive care, my first real crash after the brain injury, when I struggled with suicidal thoughts. It was like the time I wanted to drive my car off the bridge over the Missouri River, when I found out I was pregnant and was terrified our baby would have major heart problems like Daniel."

"I stood looking out the seventh-story window of the hospital room, just battling back and forth for hours and hours, agonizing, strangling with the pain, drowning in a well of grief, telling myself, 'If I jump, I won't have to feel this pain anymore.' I stayed up until three o'clock in the morning, just wanting to die, to escape, any escape at all would do."

"And I was mad. So very mad at God. I argued with Him, over and over I wrestled with Him. 'How could you let this happen, why didn't You just take him at birth, why did You let him and let us go through all these heart surgeries, do so well, and then end up like this? How could You do this? I don't understand, this doesn't make any sense at all! You are not the God I know and love. The God I know and love would not do this to me or to my son.' I was totally done in, exhausted, terribly depressed and devastated."

"The next morning God sent His angel to minister to me in the person of a godly man from our church out in Warrenton. Don Meyer came very early, around seven or seven-thirty. He had multiple problems of his own, he was crippled, he was severely bent over and had serious health issues his entire life. He looked at me and said straight as an arrow, 'The Lord gave me this passage of Scripture for you. I could barely wait for the sun to rise so I could get over here and give it to you.'"

"God's timing was so perfect. Not a single person was there with us, which was extremely unusual. There were hundreds of people at the hospital; every day and night someone was there. But not that morning - no one was there but Jay, me, and this man."

"He shared Ps. 41 with us, and the part that resonated all over my exhausted, ravaged body, soul and spirit was, 'Blessed is he who considers the weak, for the Lord will deliver him in the time of trouble. The Lord will preserve him and keep him alive, and he will be blessed on the earth. He will not deliver him to the will of his enemies; the Lord will strengthen him on his bed of illness. He will sustain him on his sickbed.' Then this gentleman, this angel-messenger from the Lord, looked us directly in the eye and declared, 'I know the Lord gave that to me to share with you.'"

"God used that Scripture to comfort our hearts, to give us hope relative to Daniel. And He sent His Word via a messenger who had been on a sickbed, who knew the trials of a broken body, so we could not dismiss or minimize the Truth this man was living. Eventually we put that passage on our license plate when we got our handicapped van. It became our rhema at the hospital, the Scripture the Holy Spirit used to barricade our spirits whenever depression pounded on our door."

"Shortly after that time God directed me to Ps. 40. It says, 'I waited patiently for the Lord and He inclined to me and heard my cry. He brought me up also out of a horrible pit, out of the miry clay, and set my feet on a rock and established my steps. He put a new song in my mouth, of praise to our God. Many will see it, and fear, and trust in the Lord.' This is the verse, the promise from God, that got me through terrible times, times when I saw no light at the end of the tunnel, times I was sure I would never survive because the pain was killing me."

"It's been thirteen years since Daniel's brain injury, and Ps. 41 and Ps. 40 are two passages I continually return to again and again. To this day they continue to speak to me, to be alive and effective in my life."

Our God of The Word

"To this day, they continue to speak to me,
to be alive and effective in my life."

The Word of God as revealed by Him to us in the Bible has always been a solid Rock upon which Susan, Jay, and Daniel can stand. It was especially so during the first four months after Daniel's brain injury.

God has given us His Word because He knows that it is the written vehicle for our relationship with Him. He also knows that the tremendous pain and the terrible groaning that characterize this fallen world and our own sin-natures would destroy us without Him and His Word to give us life. He tells us that His Words are a Lamp to our feet, providing light and direction that is unavailable elsewhere. As Michael W. Smith writes in his beautiful song, <u>Ancient Words</u>, they resound with His own heart, they strengthen us, they change us, they energize us, they help us cope.

God tells us to <u>use</u> the Word to come to <u>Him</u>, not to an experience, or a feeling, or a frame of mind, or even to another person, a friend. He tells us to go through the Word to Him, to the Person of God, to Jesus Christ Himself. His Word is a transport Vehicle that carries us to His Arms, to His Lap, to His Love, to Him. What an unspeakable joy it is to begin with Words to us FROM Him and end up embraced BY Him! His Words take us there.

God's Words belong inside of us, just as much as the breaths we take or the beating of our hearts, part of the warp and woof of the fabric of our lives. We need to hear them sounding in our heads in a deep, peaceful voice, familiar, never new or strange, like the gentle lapping of the tide upon the shoreline.

The only way to experience such imperturbable peace is to hide God's Word in our hearts, working diligently with earnest, willing sweat to meditate and cooperate with the Holy Spirit as He anchors them solidly and deeply within us (Ps. 119:11). Meditating helps us memorize new Words and retain former Words. Strong's Concordance notes the Hebrew word for meditate is *hagah*, which means "to murmur in pleasure (or anger), to ponder, to speak, study, talk, utter or mutter."[12]

Some of us are accomplished mutterers! Webster's Dictionary defines muttering as "uttering sounds or words indistinctly or with a low voice and with the lips partly closed."[13] Many of us have muttered in displeasure, criticism, sarcasm or anger. What a delightful idea to mutter God's Word in pleasure as an aid to memorizing and hiding it in our hearts! We can mutter God's Words in waiting lines in the grocery store, in doctor's offices, on hold on the telephone, anywhere we have a "waiting" moment. I mutter Scripture verses I've already memorized and want to review while I pedal the elliptical at the fitness center. My guess is that the people exercising next to me conclude I'm talking to myself, or maybe they induce I'm looney. Either way I win because of what God's doing in my heart and spirit as I mutter His Word. The strength, the security, the benefits I reap are directly proportional to the time and effort I spend hiding God's Word in my heart.

Jesus promises that the Holy Spirit will remind us of everything Jesus has said, but He does not force us to receive His Word (John. 14:26). We must make the choice. Our God of the Word strengthened Susan and Jay and helped them survive insurmountable obstacles in their lives with His Word, and He longs to do the same for you and me. Thank You, Lord!

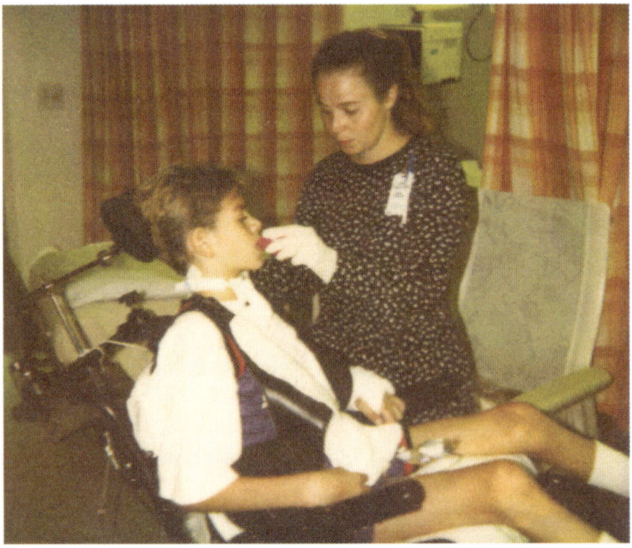

Linda gives Daniel his first drink with a cup.

"I have loved you with
an everlasting love..." Jer. 31:3c

CHAPTER 16

Signs of Love

"From the very beginning," muses Susan, "from the time Daniel was first injured, it seems God made a special point of strewing signs of His love all over our lives. He knew there was simply no way we could survive unless He continually reassured us of His love and His power, unless we were sure He was right there in the thick of the dense fog in which we were standing. So often we could see no way out, no solutions, we simply didn't know what to do and saw no light at the end of the tunnel. That's when He'd show us one more sign of His love for us."

"I remember so clearly the day my friend Jan told me the following story. She didn't find out about Daniel's injury until Wednesday evening of the day it occurred. But when she woke up on Wednesday morning, she had an overwhelming compulsion to pray for our family, and especially for Jay. She knew it was from the Lord, and she didn't understand why, but she prayed anyway. She prayed for Jay as the spiritual leader of our family and our physical provider. She continued to experience that intense compulsion all day long. Then when she heard what had happened to Daniel during surgery, she understood. It was such an encouragement to me to know that God had raised up a prayer warrior for us even when we had not asked for one ourselves."

"Then there was the time my girlfriends, who knew I really like Steve Green, the Christian singer, came to the hospital to pick me up and take me to a concert he was giving two hours away. I didn't want to leave Daniel, but Jay thought it would be good for me. It was wonderful, and really perked me up."

"While I was at the concert, my cell phone buzzed. It was Jay, telling me Daniel had talked, had said his very first words since his injury. They had capped his trache, and taken him down to therapy. The therapist told Daniel, 'Now I can hear your voice.' Daniel said 'I can too!' He said it out loud, clear as a bell, two therapists heard it."

"It gave us such hope, such joy, it was so energizing and exciting for us! But those were the only words he spoke. I remember asking Jay about a week later why he thought the Lord allowed Daniel to say those three tiny words. Jay said he thought it was a little gift to us, a little sign so we wouldn't give up hope that Daniel would one day talk again. It would be two more years before Daniel said his next words, but those words that day were a sign of God's presence and love for us just when we needed them."

"We discovered those three words were also the vehicle God used to keep the therapy team from giving up on Daniel and sending him home. Daniel wasn't progressing, he had no leg control, no muscle control whatsoever, he could do nothing. They were preparing to send Daniel home with full-time nursing care or suggest a step-down facility such as a rehabilitation home. Daniel had been getting therapy, but not intense therapy like the other children who had brain tumors, had been hit by cars, or had seizure disorders. After he spoke those three words, the whole protocol changed to one of intense therapy six hours a day, seven days a week."

"Another sign of God's love came to us through Dr. Payne. He had seen many cases where marriages break up, not because the couple doesn't love each other, but because of the strain of the stress on the marriage when a child is seriously sick or severely injured. He told us we needed to get a Christian counselor to talk with about our situation. So we did. We went to that counselor for three-and-a-half years. He was incredible. He encouraged us to get away together every few months for three or four days to regroup, figure out who we were as a couple, and remember why we had gotten married. We did that, and it was wonderful, extremely helpful."

"Dr. Payne is also the one who told us how important it was

for us to get away from the hospital on a daily basis, or we wouldn't be able to physically and emotionally survive the stress in the long haul. Of course, I didn't want to do that, I wanted to stay near Daniel. I couldn't seem to make that break myself. So our friends took over. They would come to the hospital and say, 'We are spending the night, you get out of here.' When we came back in the morning they all looked so haggard because Daniel had been screaming and crying all night, but there was nothing they could do for him. There was no way to calm him or soothe him. He didn't even know what he was doing and today he cannot remember that time at all, thank God. Our friends took turns coming but the fact that they were willing to come at all was such a potent sign of God's love to us."

"A friend of ours named Ann was the Director of Children's Miracle Network. She lived just five minutes from the hospital, and gave us access to an upstairs bedroom in her home where we would spend the night. It was so good to be away from the hospital! Some nights we would sleep well, other nights we didn't sleep at all. I remember waking up in the mornings and getting in the shower. I would turn the water on and just stand there weeping, telling God I needed someone to pray for me because I just could not go back into that hospital one more day and watch our son suffer."

"Some days I simply could not pray. Some days I couldn't read. There were many days when I felt as if I were hanging on by a thread, and if the Lord didn't do the hanging for me I would drop into the abyss. So many times I felt like a baby, like the Lord was carrying me and all I could do was lay in His Arms and weep."

"But I could listen to music, and that's what I needed and wanted. And so family and friends brought me music, so many CD's full of God's Words and promises. I listened to those CD's day and night and they gave me the strength to keep putting one foot in front of the other. They were one more sign of God's unfailing, ever-present love for me, signs I so desperately needed."

Our God Who Carries Us

"So many times I felt like a baby,
like the Lord was carrying me,
and all I could do was lay in His
Arms and weep."

Deuteronomy 33:27 tells us, "The eternal God is your Refuge, and underneath are the everlasting Arms." I witnessed Susan offering a glimpse of those Arms to Jordan, her five-year-old granddaughter, while we were interviewing in Susan's prayer room. Susan and Jay are raising Jordan, so she calls her "Mama." Jordan's perky little blond-haired head peeked through the opening she had slowly and quietly inched in the door-way. Urgently she whispered, "Mama, I need you to help me with this project for school tomorrow. It has to be done before I go in the morning."

"I will dear. I promise it will be done by the time you need it."

Mollified, and emboldened, Jordan inched the opening wider to accommodate her endearingly tiny body, slipped into the room and cautiously but eagerly climbed up into mama's lap. Taking no apparent notice, Susan went on talking about the topic at hand while simultaneously gathering Jordan into her arms, tenderly smoothing the afghan over her soft, sweet contours.

"Just like the Father", I thought, "ever ready to receive us when we bring our requests, Arms always open in eternal welcome, gathering us close, pressing us to His bosom, folding us into securest safety and rest."

"All is well, child," He says, "Your needs are met here. Come and rest."

Susan and Jordan's exchange reminded me of a mother and child I observed recently in a restaurant. A family of five - mom, dad, and three children - walked past our table and took the end booth. I could see them clearly but I could not hear what they were saying. The baby, who appeared to be approximately two-years-old, was making gulping, hiccupy sounds as if he had been crying quite awhile and rather deeply. Mom held him close in her lap, his tiny head resting wearily on her chest. He was sucking his thumb while mom stroked his back with slow, steady circular motions. His hiccupy sobs erupted every eight-to-ten seconds or so. Meanwhile, Mom carried on a congenial conversation with the rest of the family. Apparently there was no more to be done for the little one, and they both seemed to know it. Mom offered her continual soothing presence and the sanctuary of her arms to her babe. It seemed to be all the child needed despite his distress.

Hudson Taylor, a passionate missionary and prodigious author, speaks of his experience with the everlasting Arms of God in the final days of his long, beautifully productive life. He reports to his dear friend, "I am so weak I cannot write; I cannot read my Bible; I cannot even pray. I can only lie still in God's Arms like a little child, and trust."[14] In Isaiah 46:4 God assures us, "I have made you and I will carry you..." And indeed He does.

In his book, The Seaboard Parish, George MacDonald's secondary character, seventeen-year-old Connie, is lying helpless on a bed of pain, completely paralyzed after being thrown from Spirit, her favorite horse. As she visits with her beloved Papa, she voices a desire to die, believing she will never be well again and will be a burden to the family. She is, from her perspective, completely useless. Her beloved Papa suggests she must tell God she will be as He wants her to be, and offer her uselessness to Him as a burnt offering, her patience and submission as a pleasing fragrance rising up before Him. She must be willing to rest in His Arms and be carried like a little child. [15]

Deuteronomy 33:12 comforts us with, "The beloved of the Lord shall dwell in safety by Him, and He shall cover him all day long, and he shall rest between His Shoulders." When our

Savior wraps His arms around us, we know we have been wrapped. Some of my most reviving, restorative moments have come as I have sat in a rocker in our living room wrapped in a soft, hand-crocheted afghan, listening to recordings of "Sheltered In The Arms of God" and "Safe Within Your Arms", experiencing the reality of promises kept by those everlasting Arms beneath me and around me.

During a flight from Arkansas to Arizona I had the privilege of observing a mother with her baby in her arms in the seat next to me. Joy bubbled up inside as I observed their mutual love. The child, who was nine-months-old, intermittently grew sleepy. Her mother wrapped her arms closely around her, gathered her up beneath her chin, folded her own body around her baby's, and laid her cheek on top of her head. With no small effort, Mama rocked back and forth in the seat, lulling Maylee to sleep. Tenderness personified. God reflected and revealed. God says to you and me in Isaiah 49:15, 16, "Can a mother forsake the child at her breast? Or not have compassion on the son of her womb? Yes, she may forget. Yet I will not forget you. See, I have carved you on the Palm of My Hand."

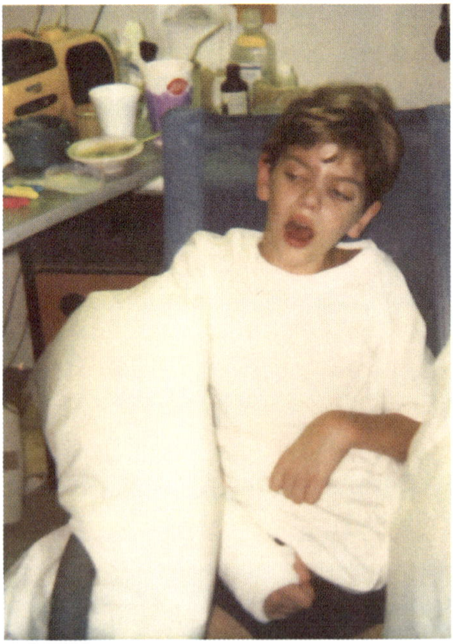

Daniel – a sitting-up milestone!

As Maylee slept on, I noticed Mama was holding up the weight of her child with her right hand. Her left hand supported her child's back as she rested against her mother's chest. The Holy Spirit reminded me of Psalm 63:8, "My soul clings to You, Your right Hand upholds me." God's spirit spoke to my spirit, inaudibly and clearly, "That's what I want you to do, Dianne, cling to Me. My right Hand upholds you just as surely as Mama's upholds Maylee. And see the sweet delight and contentment on Mama's face as she cradles Maylee in her arms? That's how I feel about you." That's how God feels about all of us. Our God Who Carries Us <u>wants</u> to do so, wonder of wonders, for the Stratmans and for you and for me! Hallelujah! Thank You, Lord!

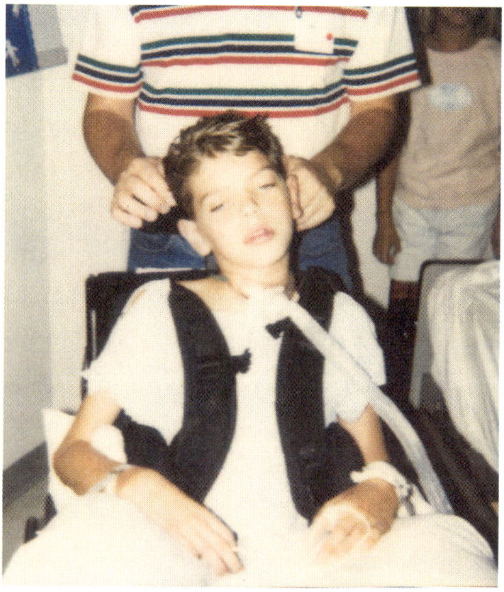

Daniel learns to hold up his head.

"If we confess our sins, He is faithful and just and will forgive us our sins..." 1 John 1:9

CHAPTER 17

When Losing Is Winning

"There were three times in those first four months after Daniel's brain injury when I took some terrible dives," says Susan. "One of them occurred after they had begun intense therapy on Daniel, six hours a day, seven days a week. Daniel was still in his agitated state, which began at the end of July and lasted into October. It was awful. He just laid in his bed, unable to speak, crying, making horrid noises in his throat, tears on his cheeks, in an agony of some kind we couldn't understand. It just about killed us to sit in that room and watch him. It ripped at my guts, it tore at my heart, sometimes I thought I'd go crazy with the grief and the pain. We could hear Daniel continually, he cried almost all the time. Everyone who came to see him would get off of the elevator and immediately hear him crying. It was horrible for us, horrible for the hospital personnel, and horrible for visitors."

"When they took Daniel down for therapy, Jay and I would take walks in this beautiful huge park across the street from the hospital, attempting to escape the haunting sound of Daniel's crying. It seemed to follow us everywhere we went. I didn't think I could take it anymore. I felt at my wits end, unable to go on. I remember having an ugly, ungrateful conversation with the Lord."

"I ranted and raved and complained and accused Him. 'Why did You let this happen, Lord, I don't understand, this isn't fair, I trusted You. You gave us a son with a heart defect, and through that I was learning to trust You, Lord. I was learning that I could put my faith in You and trust You for my life and my children's lives. Then You shattered me. I can't believe You could do this, You could let this happen! I don't know if I'll ever be able to trust You again! If I were You and I had the power You have I would heal that boy right now! Why won't You do that, why won't You just heal him? Don't You realize what glory, what power it would show? Everybody would know it was You!'"

"As I spent all my feelings and released all my ugliness on Him, I could hear Him ask, in my mind or however God does that, 'But do you trust Me now?' And I'd say, 'No, Lord, I don't, and I will never trust You again!'"

"And I'd walk some more. Jay walked beside me, but had no access to my conversation with the Lord. I argued with God. I felt like I was wrestling with Him, like Jacob did in Genesis 32. He'd wait awhile, then ask me again, 'But do you trust me now?' I could feel myself weakening each time He asked me. I began by responding, 'I'm not saying I will never trust You again, Lord.' Then, after I'd argue a while longer, I began saying, 'I WANT to trust You, Lord, but I'm so afraid because of what has happened to us.'"

"After Jay and I had walked about an hour-and-a-half, I finally stood stone-still when He asked again, 'But do you trust me now with your child?' I stood there weeping, and I surrendered. He won, and I lost - but I didn't really lose, I won. I told Him, 'Yes, Lord, I will trust You no matter what. I don't understand, and I can't believe You let this happen, but I will trust You. From this moment on, I will trust You no matter what!'" "And that was a turning point for me, a breaking point where the Lord finally got through to me. All the anxiety and fear I had pent up inside of me for the past twenty years was released. Not totally and completely, but I could feel it beginning to crumble. That incident, along with the sparrow incident and the time the man from our church brought me the Psalm 41 Scripture, seemed to work together like a battering ram to break down the stronghold of my fears. After those three times, I really didn't have any deep dives into the pit. I continued to have small ones, but no more deep ones."

"What has really touched me has been the incredible realization that God provided those three breakthroughs after I had my ugly little temper tantrums. It was always after I screamed and yelled at Him and told Him how much I hated Him and wanted nothing more to do with Him ever again that He would stoop down to show me how much He loved me. And I would feel so bad afterward. I remember confessing to a godly friend one time, ‘I just say some horrible things to Him.’ My friend said, ‘Sue, God’s big enough to handle that. He knows who you are, He knows what you’re made of.’ And I said, ‘But for Him to come down and show me how much He loves me, to talk to me in the park, to send a dead sparrow on the sidewalk, and to send a godly man to me with Scripture, how could I ever not trust Him again? After He has been so kind and loving and faithful to me, how can I not trust Him?’”

“I saw myself, I saw myself for who I really was. I saw how fragile and unreliable my emotions are, how easily I turn on Him, how wretched I really am. I have no right to question Him. He is the Creator, I am the created. I’m like a little kid stomping her foot at her parents who know far more than she does about the vegetables they want her to eat for her own good. I prefer the junk food and cannot see beyond it. God knows what’s best for me, for Daniel, for everyone. I would apologize to Him over and over, and ask His forgiveness for my ugliness. And, of course, He always gave it.”

Our God Who Wants Our Trust

> “After He has been so kind and loving and faithful to me, how can I not trust Him?”

Susan is right, of coursc - how can wc NOT trust IIim? Wc do not cause the beating of our heart - God does. Most of the time we aren’t even consciously aware that it is beating. We do not keep the world turning on its axis while we sleep. We drop off into nightly unconsciousness totally oblivious to the reality that when God wakes us up (yes, it is HE - not our alarm clock - Who has designed our bodies to waken in the morning), He has already accomplished all the significant things that needed to be done to keep the globe turning on its axis while we have been asleep. We are invited to join Him in the work He has prepared for us for the day. Then He puts us back to sleep (and out of His way!) while He continues to do all the important work of running the universe! We don't even make a choice to sleep - it overtakes us when our energies are depleted, like it or not, chosen or unchosen. God has made us that way and there is nothing we can do to change it. It happens like clockwork, like the beating of our heart. He is faithful, and the way He has made us is reliable. Is He trustworthy? Totally!

But we forget. How quickly we forget. Like Susan, we are fragile. Our feelings often rule our minds and control our lives. We forget that they are simply emotional energy, ever-changing, unreliable, sometimes reflecting reality, sometimes triggered by past experiences that have little to do with the present reality. Most of us have been led by our feelings down paths we would not have trod if we had chosen rational behavior over emotional reactions.

Our feelings are the shallowest and least meaningful dimension of who we are. Yet left unbridled, they are our most intense dimension, totally consuming our rational powers, setting our bodies aflame with pounding pulse and sweaty hands and elevated blood pressure. Our relationship with God is the deepest, most meaningful dimension of who we are and actually defines our identity and purpose. Yet many of us find that our feelings run our lives and control our behavior much of the time.

In Ps. 42:5 David asks, "Why are you downcast, O my soul? Why do you sigh within me?" Then, with mature faith that knows how to control his emotions, he refuses to allow his feelings to lead him around by the nose and undermine his peace. He commands them to "Trust in God, for I shall yet praise Him!", trumping depression and bolstering joy.

Like David, Marge Thompson is a rare person, one who has

learned to trust in the Lord with all her heart and lean not to her own understanding. She and her husband John are eighty-seven years old. When they retired fourteen years ago, they came to serve as volunteers at Glenhaven Youth Ranch, where my husband and I also do some volunteer work. John taught woodworking to the boys and did maintenance work. Marge worked as a tutor and a prayer warrior. They both shared their relationship with Jesus with the boys and the staff.

After fourteen years of service, John "retired again" because he was experiencing some disorientation and minor problems with his memory. Every morning John went for a walk in the woods on the one-hundred-fifty-acre Ranch that sits in the midst of a National Forest. Six months ago he did so and never returned home. Marge suspects he got disoriented in the woods, but no one except God really knows for sure.

A monumental search was launched for John with the National Guard, search and rescue teams from all over the state, five-hundred civilian volunteers, numerous dogs, helicopters, and air-planes. Television channels announced it. Police, hospitals, and homeless centers put up notices. Christians all over the world started praying. John has never been found.

Marge says God can be trusted, and so can His promises, especially Romans 8:28. "God works all things together for good for those who love Him and are called according to His purpose." Marge says God's purposes are bigger than the universe, and that God is using this event to save souls and touch hearts all over the world. She says God is with John on earth, or John is with God in heaven, and either way that's a win-win situation. She has great peace in her heart because she knows our God is trustworthy.

I want to grow to trust God, to learn from Him like Marge has. I want to let go of my arrogance and crucify my demands to know "why", my attitudes that say God owes me an explanation. I want to be free of the accusatory attitude that often lies hidden beneath the seemingly innocent "Why"? Francis Schaeffer reminds us that it seems profoundly unbecoming to demand anything, including answers, from our God. I don't want to behave like an unbeliever and challenge or revile God. I want to move into a posture of humility before Him. We humans have always been an arrogant, demanding people. Even in the Garden of Eden, we demanded the knowledge of good and evil, determined to know everything God knows, certain we could handle being "like" Him. Alas, it has proven to be devastatingly untrue.

Thousands of years ago after God humbled the heart of His beloved Job, Job brokenly admitted, "Surely I spoke of things I did not understand, of things too wonderful for me to know" (Job 42:3b). The Hebrew word translated "wonderful" is a primary root word, "pala", which means great, difficult, hidden, hard, too high, separate. Job acknowledges, after a wearying barrage of multiple words wherein he attempts to explain the mystery of suffering and the ways of God with His people, that he simply does not understand things that are too hard, too wonder-full, too difficult for him. He does not know or understand why God chose to permit satan to remove from him his wealth, his sons and daughters, and his health. After great angst and struggling, he finally sits still and knows that God is God and He is not. He finally stills and quiets his heart, and assumes the posture God tells us all to assume in Isaiah 30:15c, "In quietness and trust shall be your strength."

Several years after Daniel's three months in the agitated state that was so deeply devastating for Susan, Daniel retained no memory whatsoever of those horrid months of anguish. Yet for Susan they remain one of the most deeply disturbing periods of her life. It may well be that God's mercy is so great that we who observe others' pain think things are a great deal worse than do those who have to undergo them. God's promise in 1 Cor. 10:13 that says He is faithful to see that we are not tempted (and suffering is indeed saturated with temptations) beyond what we can bear is rock-solid trustworthy. He lays His Hand on us only as heavily as will be good for us. God's mercy tailors the task to suit the one toiling under it.

Our minds cannot contain the Mind of God. He created our

finite minds, and they will never grasp the infinite Mind of the Creator. God has chosen to reveal to us those things we need to know to grow in fellowship with Him. Our God Who Wants Our Trust has revealed enough of Himself and of His ways for us to be certain He is trustworthy. Thank You, Lord.

"You have been faithful with few things;
I will put you in charge of many things..." Matt. 25:21b

CHAPTER 18

Faithful

"By December, five months after Daniel's accident, I still hadn't accepted that Daniel was really brain injured," says Susan. "I kept hoping God was going to miraculously heal him. I still hope that, to this very day, fifteen years later. But at that time I desperately needed that hope."

"There were lots of people at the hospital, nurses and aides, that God used to bolster my hope and my faith. One young lady I'll never forget was named Rachel, another was Brenda. Rachel would fix Daniel's hair and say to me, 'I can't wait until Daniel can speak and tells me to leave his hair alone!' I used to tell her there would come a day when Daniel was going to walk back into that hospital and say those exact words to her. Then we'd just praise the Lord! We were faith-filled, absolutely sure God was going to do that very thing! I told Rachel, 'You know, one day we're going to have a celebration and Daniel's going to walk across the stage, and he's going to tell his story. And everyone who has ever had anything to do with Daniel is going to be there and hear his testimony.'"

"On December thirtieth, 1996, on our nineteenth anniversary, I kept experiencing nudges from the Holy Spirit to read my Bible. But I was exhausted, so I disobeyed and went to bed. Well, God woke me up at 4:00 a.m. and my first thought was, 'Read your Bible.' God never lets me get away with disobedience. I had to go to the bathroom, so I took it with me. In my Bible was my devotional, My Daily Bread, and it fell open to Dec. 30th. The title for the day was Prepare To Celebrate. It hit me like a ton of bricks. I sat there with tears running down my face. To me it was an incredible confirmation of my hope for Daniel."

"That experience has never left me. I have a card file with all the Scripture verses that God has shown me, and all the people

I want to come, and exactly what the entire celebration will look like. I've kept everything the Lord has shown me and shared with me. Maybe that celebration won't happen until heaven, but God used all of those things to bolster my faith at that time. I remember thinking about how long Abraham waited for Isaac. It was many years from the time God promised Abraham that He would give him a son to the time when that promise came true."

"At the same time that God was building my faith with thoughts of celebration, He was teaching me about the Cross, His Cross on Calvary. I was thinking about how very much I wanted to share my testimony but was worried about pride. I was wondering how people like Joni Eareckson Tada could stay so humble and obedient when so many people know them."

"God was teaching me so many things. Different people had given me three wonderful books. I had devoured them; I read them several times. They were Diamonds In the Dust by Joni, Edges of His Ways by Amy Charmichael, and A Path Through Suffering by Elisabeth Elliot. The Lord taught me so many things through those books. I wanted to teach them to others. Many people had seen and commented on our faith in the midst of our suffering. They wanted to know about the hope that was in us. We knew people who started going back to church because of our situation and other people who came to know the Lord. I knew I was just a hurting, aching mom whose flagging faith had been bolstered by the Lord, and that it was He Who held me up. So God showed me that the Cross is a place of refuge and a place of victory, but it's also a place of humility. He impressed the importance of the Cross upon me as a focus for humility. There are stick-figures prostrate at the foot of the Cross drawn in my Bible by the verses He used to teach me."

"I don't know what God will do with all of this, how He will use everything He's taught me. But I know I have to be willing to faithfully live out those things wherever I am, whether He puts me on a public platform with this book, or keeps me close at home, and whether or not He heals Daniel physically."

Our God Who Hates Pride

"I was thinking about how very much I wanted to share my testimony, but I was worried about pride."

And wisely so. God does hate pride. Prov. 16:5a tells us, "The Lord detests all the proud of heart." He knows how insidiously and how thoroughly it destroys us. God focused Susan on the Cross as a place of humility because of what happened there. The Cross is the place where our God agreed to give up His divine royalty and replace it with the nature of a servant, a decision more incomprehensible than our agreeing to give up our humanity and live the life of an ant. Our exalted God agreed to allow Himself to be made in the lowliness of our likeness, humbling Himself to participate as a human being in our mixed-up, messed-up world. Jesus could not keep both what He deserved - power, glory, majesty - and us, so He chose us! The Cross is the place wherein we discover the truth about our own depravity and need for forgiveness. The ugly truth about our fallen nature and the beautiful truth about God's willingness to suffer our consequences in our place strips away the porcupine prickles of our pride. As the Cross keeps the reality of our sin ever before us, we grow into a place of brokenness and habitual tenderness. Focusing on the Cross helps us win the enduring, ever-present battle against pride.

One of the saddest cases I know involving destructive pride is the story of John Templeton as told by Lee Strobel in The Case For Christ. John was a powerful man of God. He loved the Lord, or so it seemed. His preaching and ability to share his God with others was so powerfully electric and so seemingly authentic that through him the Holy Spirit brought hundreds of thousands to love the Father, Son, and Holy Spirit. But one day John ran into a wall he couldn't move. And because He wasn't willing to let his God move it for him, he abandoned his God. That wall was his intellectual pride, which would not bow to the Sovereignty of God.

John began ruminating about the reality of pain and suffering in the world around him. He could not intellectually reconcile that reality with our God Who is good and does good. He saw young and old, male and female, all races and nationalities struggling and straining. And he fixed his eyes on the suffering of mankind instead of on the Sovereignty of God. He forgot to glance at the problem and gaze at his God. He gazed at the problem. And he lost his way. Because he would not bow his intellect and bend his pride to a higher Mind and a greater Knowing, he gave up the One Who loved him, was dearest to him and closest to his heart. He abandoned Jesus. And he was miserable, deeply and intensely miserable, so much so that his eyes filled with tears and a deep sadness overcame him when he spoke of the beloved Friend he had abandoned.

Deuteronomy 29:29 is simple and clear, black and white, easily understood. "The secret things belong to the Lord our God, but the things revealed belong to us and to our children forever, that we may follow all the words of this law." If we knew everything, the secret things God knows, we would be as God. But we are the created, not the Creator. One of the "words" of this law instructs us to humble ourselves in the sight of the Lord. David does this in Ps. 131:1, 2 wherein he says, "My heart is not proud, O Lord, my eyes are not haughty. I do not concern myself with great matters, with things too wonder-full (high) for me. But I have stilled and quieted my soul, like a weaned child with its mother. Like a weaned child is my soul within me."

Job 11:7-9 remind us that God's ways are unsearchable and beyond the reach of our intellectual capacities even when He has given us the mind of the genius. "Can you fathom the mysteries of God? Can you probe the limits of the Almighty? They are higher than heaven, what can you do? They are deeper than hell, what can you know? Their measure is longer than the earth and wider than the sea!"

God assures us in Jer. 33:3 that He will tell us everything we need to know about His unfathomable ways if we ask Him. "Call to me and I will answer you and tell you great and unsearchable things you do not know." Inquiring of our Omniscient God with a humble heart brings guaranteed results.

C. S. Lewis speaks of the dangers of pride. After his writings began to receive wide-spread public acclaim, people began to idolize him, to place him high on a pedestal. The temptation to receive such adulation as appropriate and true is indeed great. Mr. Lewis believed we cannot be too careful NOT to think about our prideful, insidious desire for glory, lest it sneak in, worm its way through, and snare us in its incessant striving for worship, seeking to increase and enlarge our own reputation and blow up our own ego.[16]

Beth Moore offers comfort. She says that when we are feeling prideful and self-righteous, smug and superior, we need to quickly bend our knees and bow face down before God. He loves us so much He will not allow us to steal His glory, or even share it. He knows it's false, and isn't good for us. If we don't humble ourselves, He will do it for us (Pet. 5:5, 6)! He will break the knee we refuse to bend. Like all good shepherds whose primary concern is the welfare of their sheep, He will employ drastic measures to keep the sheep from repeatedly venturing into life-threatening danger. Then, when He has taken drastic measures, He will pick them up and carry them close to His heart.

Our God is an upside-down God Who has to demolish with divine dynamite our old perceptions of right-side up. He's an inside-out God Who tells us we have to go lower to go higher, lose in order to gain, suffer if we want to grow, die if we want to live, ask if we want to receive, and serve if we wish to be great. Our God Who Hates Pride washed His disciples' feet, stumbled up Calvary, and died serving us. Thank You, Lord.

"I am still confident of this: I will see the goodness of the Lord *in the land of the living."* Ps. 27:13

Chapter 19

The Many Faces of Pain

"I wasn't the only member of our family who did not believe Daniel was permanently brain-damaged," posits Susan. "Our second daughter, Jodie, was thirteen when Daniel was injured. Two days after his surgery we asked our friends to bring the girls to the hospital so we could see them and explain as best we could what was going on with their brother. After we told them Daniel was expected to live only a few days at most, our eldest, Jayme, who was fifteen, was devastated. She broke down and cried. But Jodie just looked at us with incredulity and stated, simply and matter-of-factly, 'I don't believe this. Daniel's going to be fine.' Joy, who was nine, seemed to be in shock. She and Daniel had been best friends. The blood left her face pale-white, and she went blank, expressionless."

In the wake of daunting, tragic news, God provided an incredible blessing for the Stratman girls. A wonderful, godly family they all loved folded them into their plans for the summer. The Sardina family traveled a circuit of Christian Camps all over the country, wherein Henry Sardina was a guest speaker. The girls were with friends, they were loved and cared for, they heard God's Word preached, and they had as fine a summer as possible given their circumstances. The Sardinas returned the girls to their mom and dad on Labor Day. "Henry has a heart of gold", says Susan, "He just doesn't stop giving. He was more help to us than I can say."

Susan and Jay had been living in an apartment rented for them by the hospital so they could daily be near Daniel. Once the girls returned, homeschooling began again, with Susan and Jay alternating days in the hospital with days in the apartment. Home-schooling proved to be an extremely convenient as well as effective experience for the Stratmans. Because of Daniel's situation, they were to move five times in the next four years, a terribly disruptive pattern had the girls been involved in the public schools. In fact, they never returned to their home in Warrenton. Susan sees this provision as part of God's long-term plan for them. Years earlier when Susan and Jay agonized over whether or not to home-school, God knew that it would give the girls stability through the upheaval of numerous moves years later.

"People would ask me, 'How are the girls doing with all of this?' Sometimes we took them to counseling with us, because that was a concern for us as well. I would tell people that they seemed to be doing okay, but we wouldn't really know until they were adults looking back on this time, reflecting on their responses to it."

"That proved to be true. Three years later, when Jayme was away at college about six-hours from where we lived, I received a disturbing e-mail from her. 'Mom, I can't do this God-is-love stuff anymore. Everybody here talks about a loving God, a gracious God, a merciful God, but that's not the God I know, because a loving God would not let this happen to my brother. And so, I'm telling you right now, I want nothing more to do with Him. I'm going to do what I want, I'm going to live the way I want. I don't want anything to do with God anymore.' We were just heart-sick."

"Jay and I agreed I should go down with my sister-in-law the next weekend and visit Jayme at school. We arrived on Friday, and Saturday we had a good day together. Saturday evening, when her aunt and I went back to our hotel around 10 p.m., I told Jaymie I'd pick her up for church the next morning. When I went to the dorm, she wasn't there, and we couldn't find her anywhere. My heart was aching for her."

"Things got worse. In February she turned nineteen, so we all went down to school to celebrate for the weekend. We found out she had spent her nineteenth birthday in jail, picked up as a DUI. It was horrible."

"We talked with our friend, Henry Sardina, and he suggested we take the girls, with a friend for each, on a trip for spring break. So we did, and we had a blast. Jayme went back to school to finish her semester. I picked her up at the end of the semester, and she was awful, just really mean to me. She left home after a few days, saying she was going back to Tulsa to stay with a girlfriend for a week. While she was there, she called us to say she was pregnant."

"There are different kinds of pain; it wears many faces. Pain is pain and heartache is heartache, and they all hurt so bad. But this pain was different. It was chosen, our daughter was turning her back on the Lord volitionally. Nothing had "*happened*" to her. She chose this."

"As Jay and I lay in bed that night, I thought terrible things about him. 'Why didn't Jay do this, he should have done that,' on and on. I kept blaming him. I didn't know what he was thinking or feeling. There might as well have been a wall of bricks between us. I finally said to him, 'Well, we made it through Daniel, but this stuff with Jayme could be the demise of our marriage.' I'll never forget what this man of God, my husband, whom God had chosen for me, said to me. 'Sue, it could be, but we're not going to let it be.'"

"That's all I needed to hear. It took away my burden about our marriage and my resentment toward my husband. It relieved my fears about what we were going to do. The Lord used that to give me the reassurance I needed that we were going to be okay."

"Jayme's pregnancy was a huge wake-up call for her and for us. It was a stop-you-in-your-tracks, a break-your-leg kind of thing."

"We still had mountains to climb. Jayme '*begged*' us to let her have an abortion. She knew exactly what abortion was and she knew it was wrong. And legally she could have had one anytime she wanted. She knew what the laws were. I told her that it was her choice, and I was not going to stand in her way. And thank God, she didn't choose to do that."

"Jayme planned to give her baby up for adoption, and I walked through that process with her. When she was eight-months pregnant it was time to choose a family for her baby. Jayme had previously asked Jay and me if we would adopt her baby. We prayed about it, talked about it, and told her that it was our last option. We preferred she choose another family or keep the baby herself. So she began the process of choosing a family."

"But that was not to be. She went for an ultrasound and found out the baby was a girl. We came home and went in to tell Jay, who had just returned from teaching. I'll never forget the look on his face when Jayme told him the baby was a girl. Later, when we were alone, with tears in his eyes, he said to me, 'Sue, that baby girl is a Stratman, and I have to know that baby girl will have the opportunity to come to know the Lord. We can't let her go!' The next morning he took Jayme out for breakfast and told her our third choice had become our first choice. She was so thrilled, so excited!"

"But that was not to be, either. We did go through the process to adopt her, but two weeks before we were to go to court Jayme couldn't go through with it. So we became Jordan Leigh's legal guardians, and that's how it stands today. Jordan is an indescribable blessing to all of us and her best friend is Daniel. I don't know what he'd do without her. It's just one more chapter in God's limitless, life-giving book of grace."

Our God Who Gives Beauty For Ashes

"People would ask me, 'How are the
girls doing with all of this?'"

At the time of Daniel's injury, Susan didn't realize that a disability of any kind in any family member is a disability for every member of that family. One lovely summer I had the delightful privilege of hosting a workshop for siblings of a brother or sister with a disability. It was an eye-opening, ennobling experience. I emerged from that workshop with a new category added to my list of people I admire.

Families experience incredible stress and strain as they struggle to survive the ramifications and implications each of them must face when one member has a disability. Failed marriages and family hostilities are often the end-product of that stress and strain.

Most of us willingly engage in the blame-shame game. We seem to do it automatically, naturally, and it takes great effort combined with firm resolve not to engage in that insidiously destructive game. Susan found that to be so with Jay. Eighty-percent of marriages that go through experiences with a child with a moderate-to-severe disability or extreme, disruptive rebellion do not survive, far exceeding the mainstream norm of fifty-to-sixty percent. The stress and strain on all fronts – physically, emotionally, spiritually, financially – seem to overwhelm and erode relationships. The key to survival appears to lie in what Jay so ably voiced – a firm resolve to cooperate with God's grace and disallow that erosion. God has all the grace we need, supplied exactly when we need it, to keep us going and get us through the tougher times. I remember the first time I heard the sufficient-grace phenomenon described as the "grace-of-the-moment".

My friend, Del, had a young neighbor with three small children, ages seven, five, and four. Sally had stage four, terminal cancer. She was peaceful, joyful, and optimistic as the clock ticked off the minutes of her remaining days of life. Del asked Sally how she could be so calm knowing she would be leaving her children behind, and wondered if Sally knew what she would tell her children as she became unable to function. Sally looked at Del with an enigmatic smile and gently responded, "I'm not worried about that yet. I don't have the grace-of-the-moment God will give me when I need to tell them."

Jesus makes just such a promise to His twelve disciples as He trains them, teaching them to go out among the people to share with them God's incredible love for them. He instructs them to heal the sick, raise the dead, cleanse the leper, and drive out demons. Former fishermen and a tax collector, they are deeply daunted by their lack of education and training as teachers and speakers. Feeling totally inadequate, they are greatly concerned when Jesus warns them they will be brought before governors and kings as witnesses of God's amazing love for them.

Jesus knows their timid hearts. He understands their worry about what to say and how to say it to men of high-standing in powerful places. He knows they feel like fish-out-of-water. So He assures them explicitly and simply, "...do not worry about what to say or how to say it. At that time you will be given what to say..." (Matt. 10:19b,c). The grace-of-the-moment will be theirs.

Moses had a similar experience. Terrified at the thought of appearing before Pharoah as God's spokesman, knowing it could put his life at risk, he stalls and stammers and argues with God Whom he dearly loves and Who has already shown Moses the power He will display to Pharoah via signs and wonders. Moses doesn't trust his own competency, and reminds his God – Who already knows – that he is slow of speech and tongue, unable to speak with eloquence and persuasion. God assures Moses that the grace-of-the-moment will be his, reminding him that the God Who formed our mouths and makes us deaf or mute will go with him and teach him exactly what to say when it is needed. The grace-of-the-moment will be his (Ex. 4:11,12).

Sometimes the grace-of-the-moment comes in applying general knowledge to a specific situation. Susan needed to know – but didn't know - what Jay was thinking or feeling. Susan is a strong extrovert, someone who likes to share her thoughts and feelings with others. Doing so energizes her, and seventy-five percent of our population as well. Jay is a strong introvert, someone who is de-energized by interacting with others, talking, sharing thoughts and feelings. He is energized in the quiet, in thinking things through thoroughly before he speaks, if and when he speaks at all, along with twenty-five percent of our population. As a friend conveyed to me, an introvert can sit under a tree with a true friend without saying a word and walk away feeling he's had the best conversation in the world. The introvert is energized by the inner world. The extrovert is energized by the outer world. Failing to understand that phenomenon of extroversion/introversion creates miserable misunderstanding and deep division in relationships, especially when acerbated with the stress of disabilities. Even for extroverts, sometimes things that happen to us retreat deep inside where no one goes but us and God, below the talking level, too profound or too painful for words that simply won't suffice.

The grace-of-the-moment often supplies wisdom when we need it most. Jay's words as the spiritual leader in their home were the means God used to comfort and quiet Susan's anxiety. Our husbands need our prayer. We can pray for them to grow in their role as spiritual leaders and heads of our families, and pray as well for our own understanding and ability to trust God to lead them.

Oftentimes the grace-of-the-moment doesn't look like grace at all. Jesus portrays Himself as our Shepherd in the Scriptures. God gives us images in the stories and poetry of the Bible for the purpose of helping us experience relationship with Him. Approximately one-half of the Old Testament is in poetic form, filled with rich symbolism and vivid imagery. Phrases such as "like a weaned child" and "hold you in the Palm of My Hand" help us assimilate and absorb God's tender mother-love for us. God taps into the imagination He has created in us to draw us closer to Him. The metaphor of shepherd was widely understood by many folks in an agrarian society, though that is not true today.

A shepherd does everything within his power to keep the sheep within the boundaries he has set for their safety. When one of them escapes, he goes after it and searches until he finds it. If the sheep is injured, he carries it home on his shoulders and tends it with loving care. If an incorrigible sheep continues to escape the boundaries set for it, the shepherd is actually willing to use the extreme measure of breaking the sheep's leg in order to keep it safely corralled from the life-threatening dangers of wolves and lions and poisonous snakes. Sometimes love requires drastic measures that outwardly appear cruel and intolerable, but are in reality designed specifically for our safety and well-being by the One who loves us most. Susan refers to Jayme's pregnancy as a break-your-leg wake-up call. Jayme was straying far from her Shepherd.

Straying from the Shepherd, rebelling and doing what we

want to do instead of what God designed us to do, always, always, always brings grief to us and the folks who love us. Just as putting water in the tank of a car designed for gas interferes with the purpose and plan of its designer, so does living by our will instead of God's will interferes with the plan and purpose of our Designer. As we spiral down the path that leads to trouble, repentance, and mourning, we can know with deep assurance the truth of Is. 61:1a, 2c, 3a. "The Spirit of the Sovereign Lord is upon Me (Jesus)…to comfort all who mourn…to bestow on them a crown of beauty instead of ashes…"

Regardless of the drastic measures required, or the lengths to which the sheep wander, our God Who Turns Ashes To Beauty is at work in the midst of the mess. Jayme's heart was enlarged and her character strengthened as God provided the grace she needed to turn her life around. She currently serves families as a registered nurse in the pediatric-intensive-care unit of a hospital in Arizona. Her experience with Daniel has created a core of compassion deep within her out of which she serves folks who are going through heartbreaking experiences with their little ones. Jayme has been there. She knows. The compassion that seeps from her is the same compassion that seeps from the Savior.

And of course, in this situation the coup-de-grace of our God Who Turns Ashes To Beauty resides in the exquisite, unspeakably precious gift of Jordan Leigh Stratman, now eight-years-old and a wonder to behold. Thank You, Lord

Daniel with sisters Jayme, Jodie, Joy, Jordon

"Jesus replied, 'You do not realize now what I am doing, but later you will understand'" John 13:7

CHAPTER 20

Choosing Trust

"Our second daughter, Jodie, made an ultimate choice in response to Daniel's disability that was a great relief to all of us. She was thirteen when Daniel became disabled, and her immediate response had been to refuse to believe anything permanent was wrong with him. The summer Jodie graduated from high-school was also the summer of Jayme's pregnancy. Those were rocky months for Jodie. She was initially making some choices that we weren't happy about. We were worried. Jodie's best friend was Erica Sardina, so we asked if the Sardina family would allow Jodie to go with them again as they traveled from camp to camp. Jay, Joy and I were going to be in Connecticut for several months with Daniel, to expose him to some therapy there. The Sardinas were happy to have Jodie."

"Jay and I spent July and August asking God to work in Jodie's heart so she would not choose the same path her sister had chosen. We really wanted her to go to Emmaus for a year of intense Bible Study, but she didn't want to do that. In August, the day before Emmaus began its fall semester, Jodie called to ask Jay to check and see if she could get into Emmaus. That was a clear answer to prayer."

"One of Jodie's assignments that first semester was to write a paper on an event that had changed her life. She chose to write about a young man with whom she had grown-up. He had been killed in a car accident just a month earlier. Jodie wrote that Matthew's death, Daniel's disability, the path Jayme had chosen and the fact that her parents had 'shipped her off' with the Sardinas made her stop and look at her life. She didn't understand why her friend was taken in an accident or why her brother had been injured, but she was going to go God's way even though she didn't understand. Jodie has done just that and never regretted it!"

"God brought a wonderful, Christian man into Jodie's life shortly after she made her decision to follow His plan. She married Grant in June 2006. As soon as we met him, we knew there was something very special about him. I told Jodie before we met him the first time that I had a 'test' set up for Grant that would reveal his character to me, and I would know whether or not he was a godly man. I wouldn't tell her what it was until after I met him. Then I would tell her what it was and whether he passed or failed."

"I watched Grant very carefully when he met Daniel, to see how he treated him. The test revolved around his response to Daniel. Would he treat Daniel respectfully, as a human being, or would he shun him? Would he deal with Daniel well and comfortably, or would it be too awkward for him to handle?"

"Grant passed that test with flying colors! He was sincere and compassionate, and Daniel will tell you emphatically that his best friend today is his brother-in-law!!"

"Joy, our third daughter, made choices in response to Daniel's disability that were characteristic of her entire life. She has never given us any trouble. She has been compliant and faithful, a close friend to her brother. Whereas the other girls left for college, she was at home. She has been our number-one caregiver after Jay and me. She's the one who had to live in a fish-bowl with nurses in the house during her entire adolescence. It was hard for all our teenage daughters to always have someone here."

"When Joy did go off to Emmaus Bible College two years ago, she had to write the same essay Jodie had to write about an event that changed her life. She did write about Daniel's injury, but she also wrote a comparison of her two sisters' choices and the paths they had taken. She was very thankful to have role models go before her. Joy contrasted what Jayme had gone through because of her choices, and the blessings God had given Jodie."

"Joy also wrote that she had been very mad at God. She described the anger she felt when she went to summer camp as a counselor at age fourteen, and Daniel's friends were all there. They were sixteen-years-old, working as staff, as counselors and life-guards, but her brother wasn't there. But when she looked at her two sisters, both of whom were also angry with God, she decided she was going to choose the path of obedience, God's way. She has never regretted that choice."

Daniel has three sisters, all of whom felt anger at their God and who had to make choices about how to handle that anger. All three have learned and grown because of it. Anger is a potent teacher, revealing many things to us about ourselves, not only in nightmarish tragedies like the Stratman's, but also in our lesser annoyances and irritations. It has been said that we generally reveal the depth of our character, the kind of person we are, by the things that anger or annoy us. And those things are usually inconveniences related to our own comfort and expediency, things like someone not doing what we want them to, a driver cutting in front of us on the highway, or someone taking the last piece of cake on the dessert table in the cafeteria. We seem to feel we deserve "better" treatment. We want to assert and claim our rights. But our Jesus humbled Himself, gave up His rights, and chose lesser treatment, a chance to die to Himself that we might live. We can do the same. In inconveniences and irritations that we encounter daily, or in greater life issues like the Stratman girls faced, we can choose to humble ourselves, yield our rights, and trust our God's Word which says that later, we will understand.

Our God Who Chooses To Reveal Himself

"...she was going God's way even though she didn't understand."

Jodie's choice to trust God and walk closely in relationship with Him, despite her anger and the fact that she could not decipher with her intellect the reasons for God's choices, brought her into a place of peace that passes understanding. It opened wide the doors and corridors that lead into a deeper walk of love with Him. Such choices will do the same for all of us.

To know God is to trust Him. He reveals Himself to us for that very purpose, knowing that once we comprehend even tiny glimpses of Who He is we cannot help but trust His total goodness. And once we experience His trustworthiness, we most assuredly will fall in love with Him. That love moves us into adoration, for He is truly altogether lovely, beautiful beyond description, marvelous beyond words. To adore God is to experience many things, to enter into the stillest, deepest crystalline peace available to man or woman, yet at the same time experience exultant, intensely exhilarating ecstasy. His presence soothes yet burns like a consuming fire, enthralls and empties us of self, makes us fully His. It takes one to the very edge of existence, to the point beyond which we would explode into a zillion pieces, within which there is everything and beyond which there is nothing, for all is consummate in Him. Our hearts are ravished, borne away with joy, transported with delight, enraptured by the beauty of His altogether Loveliness. We pass into His Loveliness, become united with it, are consummated by it, receive it into self, yet lose ourselves within it. Mystery is experienced.

When we emerge from worship with renewed minds and transformed hearts, as does the butterfly from the cocoon, the questions just don't matter anymore. The "whys" are lost, absorbed within the "Who". We have seen, known, loved, experienced Our God Who Chooses To Reveal more of Himself to us in worship. We are nearer than we were before. There is more of Him and less of us. We discover this is all that really matters.

We also discover that God is the great Economist Who wastes absolutely nothing. When our son Matthew went home to heaven, his sister Kathleen was nine-years-old. When she was fourteen or fifteen, folks began referring young people who had lost a brother to her, knowing they were partners on the path of pain. Kathleen was able to weep readily with them in their loss, as only one can who has been there. Likewise, Jayme, Jodie and Joy will be used mightily by God to minister as wounded healers to others who need God's compassionate and loving touch. Edwin McNeill Poteat describes it with a verse.

He cannot heal who has not suffered much,
For only Sorrow, sorrow understands.
They will not come for healing at our touch
Who have not seen the scars upon our hands.[17]

It's interesting that the Stratman girls were not angry with the anesthesiologist, but directed their anger to the One they knew was in charge of Daniel's life. They also knew, through God's revelation of Himself to them, that God was gracious and loving enough to understand their anger, despite their accusations made against Him.

We build a wall of brick between ourselves and God when we choose to anger at His choices for us. I remember well the pain of distancing myself from God when our second baby died before she could survive outside my uterus. We had already lost our first baby, and the second seemed to break the dike of my emotional endurance. I want to grow beyond that, to respond to God and to others in the way the Amish families responded in Lancaster, Pennsylvania, when their children were gunned down in the tragedy at West Nickel Mines School in October of 2006. Whenever Amish persons are killed or injured in traffic accidents, their surviving family members go to the responsible person and express forgiveness. That was true on October 2, 2006. Their Christian witness to the central message of the gospel of Jesus Christ shocked the world. They responded with submissive trust and humble resignation toward their Creator, and forgiveness and blessing toward their attacker.

It was anger that brooded and seethed in the heart of Charlie Roberts in 1998 at the death of his first child. Prematurely born in the midst of Amish country, she struggled twenty minutes before her breathing stopped. Through the following seven years Charlie nursed his anger at our God, while it metastasized and spread intoxicating tentacles both wide and deep, attaining proportions he could not control. Anger does that to us if we make choices to leave it unresolved. Six Amish children died and four were wounded in that school before Charlie's anger turned the gun on himself and took his life as well.

Mourning without anger, acceptance in the face of God's

sovereignty and mystery, an attitude of gratitude rather than entitlement, all these combined to allow the newly bereaved Amish parents to invite the family of Charlie Roberts to the funerals of their children and to welcome his wife and children to remain in and be supported by their community.

It seems God's greatest risk when He creates each human being lies within His choice to allow us the freedom to make our own choices. Yet it's the only milieu in which relationship can thrive. The bottom line in making healthy choices relative to anger or any other issue appears to be contingent upon the quality of our relationship with Jesus Christ, our choice to trust or not to trust Our God Who Chooses To Reveal Himself to us. May we choose wisely, Lord.

Daniel having fun with Jodie and Joy

"Forget the former things; do not dwell on the past.
See, I am doing a new thing! Now it springs up;
do you not perceive it? I am making a way in the desert
and streams in the wasteland." Is 43:18, 19

Chapter 21

A New Way For Daniel

"The first anniversary of Daniel's injury was approaching," says Susan. "I was finding that to be a very difficult thing. He had been released from the hospital and we were trying numerous therapies, seeking anything that might be of help to him."

"A particularly difficult stumbling stone for us came in the form of the Children's Miracle Network Telethon in May. It had been a highlight of the previous year. That entire year had been such a good one. Daniel had qualified for the select soccer team and he had the best heart check-up he'd ever had. Even with the major heart surgery, it was still a fabulous year as far as peace and health went. The Telethon had brought so much crazy fun into our lives. I wanted so badly for Daniel to be a part of it again, for our family to enjoy that fun time again. I was sure God would make a way for that to happen. So I called my friend Christine Buck, who was the news anchor for Channel Eleven, to ask her if she thought we could go again. Daniel had represented Children's Hospital in the Telethon, and he had been a poster-child for Children's as well. But, since he had been injured at Children's, Christine told me that it would be better for us not to be so visible, and said if she were us, she probably wouldn't go."

"I hung up that telephone and literally fell to my knees on the kitchen floor. I sobbed and sobbed as sorrow, marrow deep, found its familiar fit. It seemed like everything good had been taken from my life. All the fun, all the notoriety - it was a prideful thing, but it was the energy that kept me going. I just couldn't bear it. Instead of blessing me, the memories crushed me. And I had been sure God would make a way."

"When I wore myself out with the sobbing, I got up off my knees and there on the kitchen counter was the monthly newsletter from Joni And Friends. I just loved Joni. I had read every book she'd ever written, beginning with her first one in 1976. I usually just skimmed the newsletters, but this time my eyes fell on a Scripture verse that was off-set at the top of the second page. 'Forget the former things. Do not dwell on the past. See, I am doing a new thing, now it springs up. Do you not perceive it? I am making a way in the desert and streams in the wasteland' (Is. 43:18, 19). I had never noticed that verse before. It stunned me. I fell to my face, I just lost it. God spoke to my spirit, 'Stop dwelling on the past, I'm doing something new, don't you see it? I'm going to make a way!!' God's presence was in my kitchen, such a strong, very real presence. He showed me that the song He had been using to shore me up all year since Daniel's injury was intricately connected to this new verse in Isaiah."

"I need to back up a minute. Three days after Daniel's injury, on Saturday, ten months earlier, some very dear friends came to the hospital to see Daniel and us. They had just gone through the earthly loss of their eight-year-old daughter. They had buried her body on Friday, two-days after Daniel's injury, so we had not been able to go. On Saturday Steve and Sandy Sanders came to see us."

"God used Sandy to give me a song that became my song in the night. I know Sandy had no idea that song would have such an impact on my life! She went up to Daniel's bed in intensive care and leaned over him and began to sing to him. 'God will make a way where there seems to be no way. He works in ways you cannot see, He will make a way for you. He will be your guide, He will hold you closely to His side. With love and strength for each new day, He will make a way.'"[18]

"I had never heard that song before. It was brand new to me. I sat there and sobbed, both for Sandy and Steve and for us. She had just buried her daughter."

"When Sandy and Steve left I began searching for that song. It became my theme song. I sang it in the morning, I sang it all day, I sang it at the hospital, I sang it while Daniel was in therapy.

In my heart I believe the verse that song is based on in God's Word, where God promises to provide a way out so we can bear the things He asks us to bear (I Cor. 10:13). For ten months it had been my faith-builder."

"And so I was sure God would provide a way for Daniel to participate in the Children's Miracle Network Telethon. But God had just shown me through Christine that Daniel would not be in the Telethon anymore. By connecting Is. 43:18 with the song God Will Make A Way, God was taking me full-circle through a whole year, assuring me that He would make a new way, He did care for us, He was faithful and in control, but it would not be MY way, it would be a NEW way, HIS way. I had to be willing to let go of the old ways, memories, and past events to make room for God to bring in new ways. So Is. 43:18, 19 has remained God's theme for me."

Our God Who Gives Songs In The Night

"God used Sandy to give me a song
that became my song in the night."

Anniversaries are terribly difficult to negotiate, and sometimes downright devastating landmarks for folks who are grieving. They somehow highlight in neon colors the truth of what we once had but no longer do. They press us down and weigh heavily on our shoulders. We need to take the necessary time to grieve them. They are often stumbling blocks about which we have to make a conscious choice. If we are willing to turn them over to the Lord, to agree with Him about His will for us, to cast our cares on Him as He tells us to, those stumbling blocks are no longer heavy rocks, but become stepping stones to higher ground. A gospel group called Poet Voices has a CD entitled Steppin' Stones that beautifully expresses this reality.

How we choose to mark our anniversaries of loss is deeply significant in our journey toward healing. I recall with mixed joy and sadness the celebration in our back yard of the first anniversary of our son Matthew's homegoing to heaven. We sent invitations to many folks who had held us up through several nightmarish years of drug abuse in his young life. It was a lovely day in May with clear blue skies and sunshine. Folks brought potted perennial flowers and small trees, all of which were planted in our yard the next day to spill their merry beauty throughout the summer months, in celebration of his presence in our lives. Even Matthew's young friends brought small petunia plants they found to be affordable. We dug many up and transplanted them to our new home when we moved eight years later. They were a healing sight, soothing our hearts and bringing both tears of joy and tears of loss throughout the years.

It is helpful to negotiate our anniversaries with an attitude of gratitude. I can remember well the first time I saw this attitude exemplified in the midst of significant loss. My husband and I went to see an elderly gentleman from our church family who recently had his leg amputated above the knee. We expected to cheer him up, to find him somewhat down-in-the-dumps. But Jim Jones gave us quite a lesson in the art of gratefulness. When we mentioned how very difficult it would be to lose a leg, Jim's immediate comment, accompanied by a sincere smile, bright eyes, and a sweet spirit was, "Oh, it's okay with me if God wanted my leg. He let me have it for seventy-two years!" We went away humbled and deeply blessed.

The intensity and power of God's presence in Susan's kitchen that morning was an incredible gift to her. He taught her how to combine the truth that He would make a way for Daniel with the reality that Susan had to be willing to give up her attachment to the past to accept the new and different way He would usher in for Daniel. God is always present both to us and in us, as believers, but we are not always aware of it. We talk about "God showing up," or "God was there that night" as if He came upon the scene or the event from somewhere far away. He has promised never to leave us or forsake us, and He doesn't. He LIVES within us, He indwells us. We can believe what He says to be true. It's just that our level of awareness of Him changes, increases and decreases as it does in all other areas of life. We are unable to fully focus on numerous realities at one time, so our level of awareness waxes and wanes.

But, thanks be to God, His doesn't. God is ever so gracious. When Sandy leaned over Daniel's bed and sang to him the truth of Is.43:18, 19 – God will make a way – she not only ministered powerfully to Jay, Susan and Daniel, but God's Word, never returning void, ministered to Sandy as well. Sandy was living in a dark night of grief at that time, as were Susan and Jay. Sandy needed desperately to be reminded that God would make a way for her and for Steve to survive that grief, to bear up under the horrible burden they were carrying. God always returns thirty, sixty, and a hundred-fold the blessings we reach out to give to others. God gave Susan a literal song through Sandy that she sang when she awakened in the night, and at the same time that song ministered to the night-time of Sandy's awful grief.

Psalm 42:8 speaks of God's graciousness in giving us songs in the night. "By day the Lord directs His love, at night His song is with me." In Ps. 77:6 we are assured that comfort is found by remembering those songs in the night. Our God Who Gives Songs In The Night is there for Susan, for Sandy, for you, and for me on the mountaintop and in the deep valley, in the daytime and in the middle of the night. Thank You, Lord!

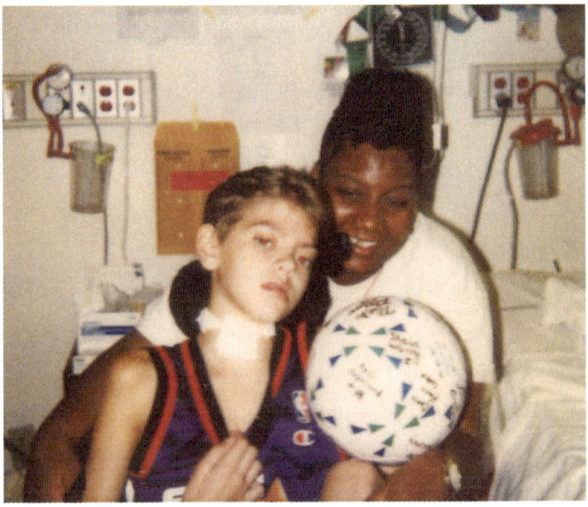

Rochelle helps Daniel keep on keeping on.

"...Weeping may remain for a night, but rejoicing comes in the morning." Ps. 30:5b

CHAPTER 22

Year of Miracles

"I kept a journal of Daniel's daily progress," reports Susan, "and at Christmastime, almost a year-and-a-half after his injury, I wanted to send friends and family an update on all that the Lord had done in our lives. Daniel had made a miraculous recovery! From the point at which we were told he would be a 'vegetable', to take him home, change his diapers and try to get on with life, to the point where he had progressed by that Christmas, an amazing series of steps had occurred. We called it our 'Year Of Miracles.'"

"When we came home from the hospital four months after his injury, he was still doing almost nothing and saying nothing. He could stay on his feet when he was positioned in a stander. But that was it."

"While we were still in the hospital I was determined he was going to learn how to eat again. His favorite food was a Steak-N-Shake burger, and pizza. I couldn't imagine him not eating those things ever again. So while the hospital personnel were feeding him through a tube in his stomach, I was feeding him little bitty tastes of his favorite cereal, Cream-of-Wheat. Sometimes the two feedings collided and he threw it all up. But I knew he would want someone to teach him to eat again, so I just kept on. I had prayed persistently that the tracheotomy tube would come out, and it did after six weeks. Then the goal was to get him to eat a certain number of calories so they would agree to take the feeding tube out. Daniel graduated to pureed food, and then to smashed-up hot dogs and mustard and ketchup. I remember Jay's good friend, Dennis Ford, just about losing it when I fed the smooshed hot dog to Daniel! By the time we went home, Daniel was eating little tiny bites of regular food. Soon after we got home, he began eating chopped chicken nuggets and pizza, and eventually everything he had ever eaten before in his life. How we praised God for that!"

"When Daniel came home from the hospital it took six people to help him stand on his feet. The girls and I, the nurse, and Jay would pull Daniel up and make him imitate walking. One person would hold one leg, a second would hold his other leg. A third person would hold onto one arm, a fourth on the other arm. A fifth person would hold his head, because he had no head control. The sixth person would try to coordinate everything. We made him move. It took about six months of daily practice, but eventually Daniel walked haltingly like he does now, with one person holding onto him."

"Daniel was getting three hours of daily therapy at the hospital, as well as speech therapy and occupational therapy here at home. A massage therapist came once-a-week. The Lord led us to an acupuncturist named Lesley, who came from two-to-three-times a week for about three years, until she and her husband moved to Georgia.

"Lesley was phenomenal! She would say to us, 'We're going to get Daniel out of diapers!' So we all worked together, and in six weeks Daniel was out of diapers! Our house must have seemed really strange during those six weeks. Daniel had a lot of trouble with bowel movements. I'd sit on the edge of the tub while he sat on the toilet. One day I noticed that if I made him laugh, he relaxed, and could have a bowel movement. So I'd tell him funny stories and jokes and when I couldn't think of any more the girls would come in and tell him jokes and funny stories. Daniel's going to the bathroom became a real family affair at our house!"

"There were lots of 'firsts' in that bathroom, and I cried so many tears of joy in there. As I sat on the tub, I'd work on consonant sounds with Daniel, 'm, d, p, f, b'. That was where he said his first syllable after his injury, 'muh'. And it was during what had become our special time together, waiting for him to go to the bathroom, that he said, 'mom'! I'll never forget that. It seemed to have been so terribly long ago that he had said, 'mom'. It was just before he walked through those double doors into hernia surgery that he had said, 'I love you, Mommy, I love you Daddy!' We never knew if we'd ever hear him say those words again. I remember telling him, 'Daniel, I will never tire of hearing you say *Mom*. You can say *Mom* as much as you want, anytime you want.'"

"Now it's become a joke. Daniel will say 'Mom' to get my attention, then he says a sentence and says 'Mom', and another sentence followed by 'Mom'. So I say to him, 'Daniel, you don't have to say 'Mom' so much.' Grinning, he reminds me I once said I'd never tire of hearing him say 'Mom'!"

Our God Who Delights in Us Delighting

> "I wanted to send friends and family an update
> on all that the Lord had done in our lives."

Susan wanted her family and friends to delight in her God, to rejoice with them in His blessings to Daniel and to their family. Susan delights in seeing others delighting. And so does our God.

God's Word tells us clearly that He is our God Who delights to give us good gifts. In Matt. 7:11 Jesus asks, "Which of you, if his son asks for bread, will give him a stone? Or if he asks for a fish, will give him a snake? If you then, though you are evil, know how to give good gifts to your children, how much more will your Father in heaven give good gifts to those who ask Him?" (The Greek word "evil" used herein, *poneros*, refers to evil in effect or influence and not to evil in essential character.) In 1 Timothy 6:17 we are commanded to put our hope in God, "...Who richly provides us with everything <u>for</u> <u>our</u> <u>enjoyment</u>."

Last month I saw such a beautiful illustration of this reality. I rode up to Dayton, Ohio, to visit the granddaughters of a beloved friend. Caitlyn is three-years-old and Amelia is one-and-a-half. As my friend and I relaxed on lawn-chairs in the back-yard, we spent much of our time on a lovely butter-yellow summer day watching these two small children amble from one pleasure to another. Caitlyn poured water from her wading pool into her water table, delighting in the doo-dads that flopped and whistled and whirred when the water reached a predetermined level. Amelia wandered over to her gym-set and leisurely but with studied purpose negotiated the ladder to zip down the bright blue slide. Caitlyn delighted in wetting our denuded feet with drops of water painstakingly transported from her pool with a shiny red shovel. A patch of brightly blooming daisies beckoned, and Amelia toddled over to watch the wind gently ruffle their soft stillness. Stooping down, she plucked a single bloom first for one tiny fist, and then the other. These little ladies had lifted not a finger to supply their treasure-trove environment. It was Mom and Dad who had "richly provided them with everything for their enjoyment." And it's Mom and Dad who delight in their delighting. In fact, that's WHY Mom and Dad provided it – for their daughters' delighting. And so it is with God, Whose image we reflect in every good thing that we do.

God reveals Himself to us as a God Who firmly established numerous days within the calendar year to be set aside for festivals of delighting. He created us in His Image. He delights. He knows we need to delight. The Jewish calendar designated literally dozens of days in which the people of God were to enjoy celebrations, to play, delighting in their God, in His gifts, recalling His faithfulness, and enjoying each other. God was so intent upon their participating in the celebrations in Jerusalem that He gave instructions relative to setting aside financial and practical provisions to be used in travel to make the journeys to Jerusalem a reality in their lives.

Playing, delighting, enjoying, rejoicing are all commanded by our God. Professor Wayne Bowen, formerly of Ouachita Baptist University, offers a sage comment relative to his four-year-old son, Sam. He posits that wee Sam has possibly uncovered the existential question underlying nearly all human transactions when he asks, "Do you want to play with me?" Professor Bowen wonders how many times he himself initiates a conversation with some other phrase when that indeed is what he's really asking.

One of the anthropomorphisms God had given us that

touches my heart most deeply with its blatant tenderness is Zeph. 3:17 adapted from the New Jerusalem translation. "Yahweh your God is in your midst, a mighty Savior. He will rejoice over you with singing. He will quiet you with His love. He will rejoice over you with dancing, as on a day of festival." The Hebrew word for singing, *rinnah*, says so much more than the numerous Biblical translations allow. It means to emit a creaking, shrill or strident sound or shout of joy. The word for rejoice is *guwl*, meaning to spin around under the influence of any violent (strongly intense) emotion. The word for joy used in the King James translation is *simchah*, meaning exceeding gladness or glee. Do you see your God that way? I struggle to do so. To reflect on the reality that our God chooses to shout with joy about me, to spin around in uncontainable, intense delight in me, boggles my puny brain. It seems incredible, untenable to me. How so? How could it ever be so?

Yet I caught a momentary glimpse of how it could be so when my friend and I sat together in those butter-yellow moments and observed two little ladies as they explored the treasures offered by their parents. We were absorbed by and delighted in their delighting, possibly reflecting a somewhat tiny similarity to Our God Who Delights In Our Delighting. Thank You, Lord.

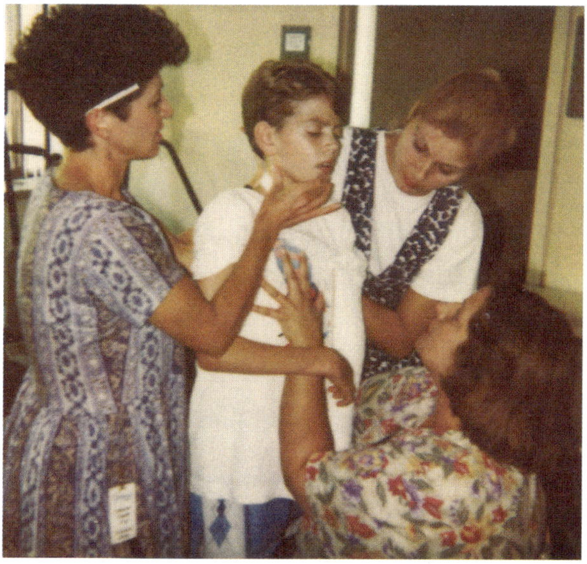

Daniel, Catherine, Amy and Theresa work on "standing up."

"...there is a friend who sticks closer than a brother." Prov. 18:24b

CHAPTER 23

Scattered Friends

Susan shares nostalgically, "At the time Daniel was injured, he had four really good friends." One of the most difficult and saddest realities for folks with severe disabilities is the hurdles erected between friends by their disability. It takes tremendous effort, much time, undaunted determination and pure grit to create or maintain a friendship with a person with severe disabilities. It has to be something we desire deeply and pursue doggedly or it simply doesn't happen, not in the lives of most adults and certainly not in the lives of eleven-and-twelve-year-old boys.

"In many ways, Daniel's disabilities isolated him, separated him from his friends. All of the boys were very athletic, and they loved to spend time outdoors together. They were fun-loving fellows. Daniel was not only unable to do all the things they used to do together, but he also could not even communicate with them. The only thing he would really do was laugh at their jokes. But that doesn't go very far in maintaining a relationship."

"In time, the relationships cooled and eventually disappeared. Daniel was primarily with his sisters and his parents. I began praying that God would send him just one good friend. And He did, in his new brother-in-law. But it's a long-distance friendship, because Grant and Jodie live so far away from us."

"So I still pray. And I also pray for a wife for Daniel. Whether or not the Lord will choose to do that, I don't know. It's probably just a selfish mother's desire for her son, but it's on my heart. I know God knows best!"

Our God Who Is Our Friend

"I began praying that God would send him a good friend."

When I interviewed Daniel for our first taping, I asked him what had endeared God most to him in the twelve years since his injury. Daniel responded, "He's everything to me." In response to a question about the advice he would give to folks who are experiencing difficult circumstances, Daniel said, "I would tell them they need to hang onto God."

In other words, God is not only Daniel's Lord and Savior, God is also Daniel's best Friend, his All-in-All, his Answer to every situation. It doesn't get any better than that. The "friend who sticks closer than a brother" is Jesus Christ, Who speaks quite plainly about where He stands in His relationship with us in John 15:15. "I no longer call you servants, because a servant does not know his master's business. Instead, I have called you friends, for everything I have learned from My Father, I have made known to you." None of us know how many hours and how much agony Jesus spent instructing His disciple-friends in their three years together, then speaking His last words and legacy to them, equipping them to go through the ordeals that lay ahead for them after their last supper together in the upper room in Jerusalem.

Prov. 27:6 tells us wounds from a friend can be trusted, and Prov. 17:17 defines a friend as someone who loves at all times. John 15:13 reminds us that there is no greater love than that which compels us to lay down our life for our friends. Jesus was just such a Friend. The only way Daniel or you or I or anyone can get into the pit of hellfire where we are eternally separated from God is to purposefully and mean-spiritedly climb over the bruised, battered, bloody Body of Jesus Christ and refuse to receive His offering to be our Savior and Friend.

God cautions us about the natural consequences that befall us when we place too much weight on human relationships. Ps. 118:8 tells us, "It is better to trust in the Lord than to put confidence in man." Is. 2:22 uses more compelling language to protect us. "Stop trusting in man who has but a breath in his nostrils. Of what account is he?"

Unlike Daniel's young friends, God's love for us isn't dependent on the way we look or whether we can walk or talk or any condition whatsoever. He first loved us, we didn't earn it, and we don't have to perform to keep it. It's pure, unadulterated gift. The only sin Jesus won't forgive is our refusal to receive that Life He laid down for us, that offer of eternal Friendship. To refuse the offer of Salvation and Friendship from Him Who first loved us is to sin against the Holy Spirit, Who teaches us all things and reveals Jesus Christ to us.

In John 14:26 Jesus tells us, "But the Comforter, the Holy Spirit, Whom the Father will send in My Name, will teach you all things and remind you of everything I have said." It is the Holy Spirit's joy to reveal and teach us about Jesus. When we stubbornly refuse to accept the truth of Who Jesus is, attribute His power to satan, and harden our hearts against Him, we commit the unpardonable sin of blasphemy against the Holy Spirit. It is the Holy Spirit's ministry to us to open our eyes, convict us of sin, and draw us to Christ. He strives to woo and win us to Jesus. But after repeated refusals and insults and despisings, the Holy Spirit ceases to strive with us and completes what we have repeatedly determined we will have, i.e., hardened hearts. Like Pharoah in his persistent refusals to obey God despite the signs, warnings, and plagues through Moses, we cross the line drawn in the sand and reach the point of no return.

It seems God has always desired to be our Friend. Difficult as it is to comprehend, our God Who is our opposite in so many ways, and to Whom we bear an unfathomable likeness, had Friendship as well as Lordship in mind when He created us. It seems God chose to walk in the Garden of Eden in the cool of the day with Adam and Eve, and He chose to walk with Enoch in Gen. 5:22. Lest we not quite comprehend the incomprehensible, Gen. 5:24 states again the reality of Enoch and God's friendship. In 2 Chron. 20:7 Abraham is identified as God's friend, and again in Is. 41:8 and Jas. 2:23. In Matt. 11:19 Jesus clearly chooses the least desirable persons, the social outcasts, the misfits and the marginal, to be His friends.

Jesus chooses you and me to be His friends. Jesus is the only Friend Who never fails to do what good friends do. The rest of us, try as we might, fail to be all that a friend should be. No wonder Daniel Stratman chose the Best to be his friend, Our God Who Is Our Friend. Thank you, Lord!

Daniel and Grandpa Dobos – friends!

"For the earth will be filled with the knowledge of the LORD, as the waters cover the sea."
Is. 11:9b

CHAPTER 24

Glorifying God

"Numerous times in the last several years Daniel has asked me,' Mom, why do you think God let this happen to me?' "

The question Daniel asks Susan embraces every part, every aspect of his multiple disabilities, and there are many, indeed. Daniel's vision has been significantly limited by his accident. The optic nerve is unaffected and the pathway to the brain is intact. But it seems the central cone has been damaged, and so Daniel sees peripherally. He can see things that are down low and off to one side. Based on testing at eye institutes in several states, it appears that Daniel has Swiss-cheese vision, spaces where he can see and areas where he cannot.

The area of the brain that processes sight is also the area that processes math and spelling. Daniel was once an outstanding speller, but no longer so. He cannot understand or decipher math.

Daniel's speech is severely limited. "The key to understanding Daniel lies in watching his lips," says Susan. "He forms most of his words correctly, but the muscles cannot deliver them. Just as you learn with a small child by being with him and discerning how he says certain words, we did that with Daniel. It's like learning another language. We've tried Braille and Dynavox and sign language and many other communication devices. But because Daniel's whole body is so severely limited, none of those worked. We are just so grateful Daniel began verbalizing, even though it was very frustrating at first. The muscles in the back of his throat had atrophied, so almost all of his vowels sounded the same. Much of our success in learning to understand him was at first like a guessing game. If you're around Daniel enough, you can pick up on it. Jodie's husband Grant, and Joy, as well as a few other people, can understand him."

"Daniel's short-term memory was dramatically affected by the injury. He has to listen to school reading-assignments on tape as many as thirty times before he can adequately remember them. But God has granted Daniel the comforting gift of preserving in his long-term memory all the verses of hymns he learned in his first eleven-years of life."

"Daniel still sings! If we sing a newer song at church, he's lost, he can't remember it. But if we sing an old song, he sings right along with us. It's a monotone, but to me it's just beautiful. I sometimes have to stop and just watch him. I get all choked up. I'm so grateful that the Lord preserved those songs for him!"

Daniel's injury affected the basal ganglia and the occipital part of his brain, which included all of his motor skills as well as his vision. Brain scans reveal holes throughout his brain wherein the lack of oxygen assaulted globally."

"But we praise the Lord over and over because it did not affect his personality. We still have our Daniel, not a stranger in his place, like many brain injuries leave behind. Daniel's long-term memory allowed him to pick up pretty much where he left off with sports, Bible knowledge, faces and names of people. If I forget a name, Daniel will know it! That's just an incredible thing to me!"

"I remember in those first months after his injury, during our year-of-miracles, how Daniel's progress from what the doctors told us would be 'a vegetable' paralleled my prayers. I would ask God to stop the horrible crying in the hospital. And in His perfect timing He did. I asked Him to give Daniel back his speech, and He did. I asked God for Daniel to be able to stand, and with help, he can. I asked for Daniel to be free of diapers, to be able to go to the bathroom. God said 'Yes.' But for so long I was confused because although God gave Daniel partial healing in so many areas, He never gave him full healing in any of them. I used to ask Him over and over, 'Why did You quit, Lord? Why did you stop short of complete healing?'"

Susan's question resonated with the inquiry of Jesus' disciples when they asked Him in John 9:2 why a man was born blind. Jesus' answer is applicable in response to any "why" we might have about any difficulty we or anyone we love may face in their lives. Jesus told the disciples the man's blindness "happened so that the work of God might be displayed in his life." Susan learned, as time passed on, that this was true for Daniel.

"I think I have learned over the years that God is more greatly glorified in the way Daniel is now than He would be if Daniel were fully healed. We met a gentleman at an assembly in Florida when we took Daniel down for some balancing therapy. When this man first met Daniel he prayed fervently for his healing. But after he got to know Daniel he shared some interesting insights with him. He said, 'Daniel, when I first met you I was sure God wanted to heal you. But now that I've gotten to know you, I'm not so sure. You have had a big impact on me. When I see you smile, hear you laugh at jokes, and see your joyful spirit in the midst of all that your body is NOT doing, I'm not sure God would choose to heal you. You are such a blessing to everybody just the way you are!'"

In a most distinctive way, God is using Daniel's injury and his life to help fill His earth with the knowledge of the glory of the Lord. "When I think of all the people who have been influenced for salvation after hearing Daniel's story and meeting him, all the children at camps, all the medical personnel who have returned to the Lord after backsliding, I can see all the ways God is glorified in this," says Susan. "I'm still not able to say 'Thank You, God, FOR Daniel's brain injury', but I am able to thank God for all the good He has brought out of it. Someday I want to be able to thank Him FOR the injury. God will help me, and some day I will."

Our God Who Is the Potter

"...I'm not sure God would choose to heal you."

The insights shared with Daniel by the gentleman in Florida remind me of the revelations God shares in His Word in Isaiah.

"Yet, O Lord, You are our Father. We are the clay, You are the Potter. We are all the work of Your Hand" (Is. 64:8). "…Shall what is formed say to Him Who formed it, 'Why did You make me like this?'" (Rom. 9:20,21).

In Ex. 4:11,12 God makes it absolutely clear that His Sovereignty embraces all things. "The Lord said to him (Moses), 'Who gave man his mouth? Who makes him deaf or mute? Who gives him sight or makes him blind? Is it not I, the Lord?'"

For years and years, over and over, Susan says she asked God, "Why? Why? Why?" It's the natural thing to do, the logical question to ask. And it's also the cause of great unrest, the source of our inability to lay our burdens down, cast our cares upon Him, and enter into rest and peace of mind.

I am reminded of an incredible woman named Anna who is living testimony to me of how to put our "whys" to rest in God's Hands. When Anna joined a grief support-group facilitated by my husband and me, she shared her heart-wrenching story wherein she learned to crucify her questions, refuse to give them a hearing, and ruthlessly subject her feelings to her higher mind, will, and the Holy Spirit's control. We live in an emotionally fragile world wherein people like Anna are rare. We indulge our feelings to a fault. We whine like Job, we pout like Jonah, we despair like Elijah, we murmur like the Israelites when they wanted meat instead of manna. John Piper says that when historians write about the character traits typical of the last third of the twentieth century, endurance and bulldog tenacity, perseverance and constancy-in-commitment will not be among them. Self-realization, self-assertion, self-esteem, self, self, self, will head the list. Not so with Anna, who is in her seventies. With tear-filled eyes, and softly-spoken words, Anna shared her story.

"I don't know what happened. No one saw it but the girls. They are so young (five and seven years), and I just couldn't make them re-live it all again by telling me, by answering my questions, just so I could know. They were in the water, both girls had their *swimmies* on, and were out paddling and kicking in the lake. Henry couldn't swim. He must have gone out to get the girls to come in, because the couple that heard them crying said they were in the water, asking, 'Where is Grandpa? We can't find Grandpa!" The couple had been on the beach, sunning themselves, a good distance from the girls. No one else was around. They heard the crying and walked over to see what was wrong. They brought the girls in to shore and called 911."

"When Henry didn't pick me up after my meeting, like he was supposed to, I began to get concerned. I knew if something had happened to the girls he would have called me. Since he didn't, I knew something must have happened to him. When he was twenty minutes late to pick me up, I asked someone to drive me to the lake. I saw all these people bunched around our car, including the police. I knew. I just knew."

"The other policeman had taken the girls down to the police station because they didn't want them to stay in the area. The girls were so upset. The police had already taken Henry's body to the morgue. In the ride down to the station I had time to pray. I asked God, 'What should I do?' I had to stay in control because I didn't want the girls to see me so upset. I knew they would already be suffering enough. God told me not to ask them any questions, to just let them tell me what they wanted to tell me. So I did. So I don't really know any details."

"The littlest one gets very sad now and says she caused Grandpa to die. I think she had paddled out too far and Henry was going after her. But I don't really know. I really don't know much at all. The girls will talk about it when they're ready. Until then, I can let it rest in God's Hands."

Many of us would tell ourselves we "can <u>not</u> wait, we <u>have</u> to know", and ask our questions, seek to satisfy our "whys" and "hows". Like Anna, Susan hopes to grow to the place in her relationship with God the Father, Son and Holy Spirit wherein she can lay aside her "whys" and wholeheartedly say without reservation of any kind, "I trust You, Lord, with all my heart. I lean not to my own understanding. Thank You FOR Daniel's injury and the truth that it is the best possible path Daniel's life could have taken, both for his sake and for everyone else's."

Susan already says that Daniel's injury has made him, shaped the depth and joy and beauty in his character, in his very being.

And that's what God is primarily concerned about – our being, our essence, our personhood. Our bodies will deteriorate and fall away, corruptible, no longer suited to our spirits and our souls. They will be buried in the ground or cremated to ashes, until the day of Jesus' return, at which point they will be raised incorruptible, restored to the original condition in which God created them. Until then, they remain dispensable and temporal, limited by the days God has designated for them.

Somehow we get that reality mixed up, and our bodies take precedence over our souls and spirits. We feed them three meals daily, often with snacks in between. We haul them to the doctor for regular check-ups and testing. We don't feed our spirits with the same intensity or frequency of care, nor our souls.

God desires our holiness, not our happiness. He is concerned with our character, not our comfort. A fully healed Daniel could become absorbed into the horde of millions of others who have healthy bodies. Certainly the living testimony he is today would disappear. Daniel might possibly become busy with earning a living, distracted by the "normal" things with which so many of us fight to be free. I'm reminded of what Joni Eareckson Tada said when she finally gave up traveling the world in search of physical healing. "Okay, Lord, You obviously have something else in mind." It would seem God had in mind Joni's presence in our needy world, her personhood, her character, her being. That's where Joni's power lies – in her presence. The degree to which God is present in Joni is commensurate with the degree to which she has suffered and grown through the disability God chose <u>not</u> to heal in her body. It's God's presence in Joni's presence, His Spirit dwelling in hers, that moves the Larry Kings and the Billy Grahams and the President Bushs to seek her out for interviews and visits. It's God's presence in Joni that brings such joy to the little, names-unknown ones in Peru and Bolivia and Mexico when she and her ministry team deliver wheelchairs to them. The glory and the miracle are bound up in the body NOT working while the spirit and soul ARE working so powerfully well! Hallelujah!

Our God Who Is The Potter knows exactly how to make that

happen, what circumstances to create within the clay in order to reveal His glory for all the world to behold. Thank You, Lord!

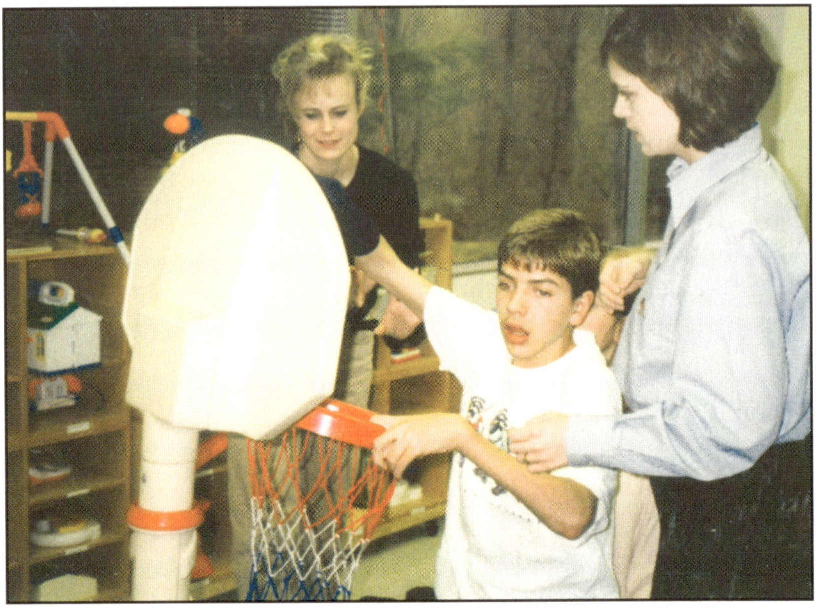

Daniel working hard at therapy.

"For God does speak... in a dream, in a vision of the night, when deep sleep falls on men, as they slumber in their beds..." Job 33:14a,15

CHAPTER 25

Daniel's Dream, Jay's Dream

A dream can be defined as a hope, an aspiration, a mental image of something that catches our fancy, something we want to pursue or cause to become reality. In his book, Hustling God, M. Craig Barnes writes that everybody has dreams, they run our lives, get us up in the morning, drive us to work, motivate us to do whatever it takes to pursue them.

The Holy Spirit refers to dreams in the Bible as commonplace phenomenon wherein God speaks to human beings, oftentimes as a vision or mental image in the night. A description of dreams that quickened my heart and has remained with me since I first heard it many years ago is found in the 1955 Cinemascope Production of A Man Called Peter from the book by Catherine Marshall. As a young man of almost thirty-years Peter Marshall discovers, much to his surprise, that Catherine is the woman God has chosen to be his wife. In a most dramatic manner, Peter grasps Catherine firmly by the shoulders and attempts to communicate his discovery to her. "Don't you know that God plants His own lovely dream in the human heart, and that when the dream is mature and the time is ripe for its fulfillment, to our astonishment and delight, His will becomes ours and ours His! Now Who but God could have thought of anything as perfect as this?"[19] Of course, Catherine already knew, for God had planted that same dream in her heart years before.

So it has been with Daniel. Susan says, "Daniel loves learning, he always has. But especially now. He has always dreamed of going to college. He is attending Emmaus Bible College, and when the semester is over, he is down-in-the-dumps. He loves to learn new things. And going to school also helps him feel productive, like he's doing something worthwhile."

When I asked Daniel, "What's the best thing God has done for you in the past fourteen years," Daniel responded, "I am finally in college. It's the best place I can be."

Daniel works hard to "be in college", very hard indeed. Susan says, "We tape the lectures while Daniel is in class. Then we play them at home, many, many times. He probably listened to the Book of Hebrews at least thirty times when he was in that class. He has to hear things repeatedly, over and over, to remember them."

I asked Daniel if he plans to finish college. He spoke emphatically, "I AM!" It will take Daniel eight-to-ten years of full-time work to accomplish what most other folks accomplish in four. But Daniel is determined.

Susan says, "He wants to do well. He has never liked mediocrity. I thank God that's one of the things that did not change when he was injured. So many times children who are brain injured experience big changes in their personalities. Daniel did not. I know someone whose son fell out of his bunk bed and smashed the front of his head. The frontal brain injuries often cause personality change. Her son can become extremely violent and when he was an adolescent they had to place him in a home. We still have our Daniel, with his personality intact. I'm so grateful for that!"

Jay also had a dream, mentioned in the first chapter of this book. Jay wanted a son with whom to continue the tradition he had established with his own father of sharing their spectator's love of sports. In 1984, when Daniel was born, Jay presumed his dream would be fulfilled. And our gracious God did indeed arrange the fulfillment of that dream, but not in quite the way Jay had envisioned.

Jay and Daniel have been blessed to visit every baseball stadium in the United States and Canada. Daniel says those events are the "most fun" things he does. Jay spends a lot of his time and energy at games accommodating his son's insistent desire to stand-up and holler at the team, either to cheer or vent displeasure. Daniel hollers, "Get me up! Get me up!" Jay grabs Daniel by the back of his belt and the waistband of his pants, hauls him upright in the stands, and holds onto him while Daniel yells away. Then Jay sits him down again until the next outburst of passion. It's quite a sight to see!

When the doctors first erroneously told Jay and Susan that Daniel was blind, "Jay just cried and cried", says Susan. "It was really hard for him. That part of it wasn't so difficult for me. But Jay must have known that would mean many things, including no more shared sports events." Yet once again our gracious God has made provision. Daniel watches games through his peripheral vision, and listens to the play-by-play with headphones, so he doesn't miss a thing!

When asked about his favorite memory, Daniel grins and says, "I finally saw the Cardinals win a World Series!" And Jay was with him, two spectators enjoying a father-son event together! Hallelujah!

Our God Of Dreams

"I'm finally in college.
It's the best place I can be."

God often provides the means to fulfill our dreams long before we recognize exactly what He's doing. Finances were a serious problem for the Stratmans. With Susan as a full-time homemaker and Jay a school-teacher, funds were greatly limited and the budget was tight for them.

"Jay was worried", says Susan. "We had bills that needed to be paid at home, and daily the bills piled up as Daniel spent week after week in intensive care and month after month in the hospital. Jay painted houses in the summers when he was not teaching school. But the painting he had planned to do went out-the-window as we spent day after day at the hospital with Daniel. I remember telling Jay that if the Lord was allowing this to happen to us, He would certainly take care of our finances."

When Jay was concerned that their finances would be

"ruined", Susan was his helpmeet, encouraging him to know that God would not let that happen. And when Susan was concerned that their marriage would be "ruined" because of all the stress relative to Daniel's injury, Jay was her spiritual leader, encouraging her to know that they would not let that happen. That's God's plan for marriage. Helpmeets, spiritual leaders, encouragers, helping each other up when one falls down – that's God's ingenious, wonderful plan for marriage. And it played out well in the Stratman's relationship.

Friends of Jay's, godly men whom he respected, well-aware that the Stratman's bills were sky-rocketing and willing to help as much as they were able, began suggesting that Daniel was going to need care for the rest of his life. It would be expensive, very expensive indeed. One of them gave them the name of a lawyer.

"We had no legal experience" Susan relates, "we had never even talked with a lawyer in the legal sense. We didn't have a clue what to do. The thought of suing the hospital had not entered our minds. The hospital had already begun paying all our expenses after the investigation ordered by Dr. Payne. That was a direct gift from God. And we knew we did not want to sue anyone. But we did go talk with this lawyer. And it became a nightmare, a fiasco for the next eighteen months. It became so clear that all the lawyer really cared about was how much money he could possibly get from the risk-management people."

"After a year-and-a-half of craziness, after prayer, and fasting, and seeking godly counsel, we fired the lawyer. Meantime, three different folks had given us the name of another lawyer who was known for his honesty and integrity. Jay was so disillusioned, he just wanted to drop it. He kept saying, 'We don't need this nightmare, let's just drop it.' We knew the Lord would take care of Daniel, one way or another. God is God, He can do whatever He wants, however He wants."

"We have a good friend who is close to thirty years-old now, whose name is Brad Sanders. He was born dead. Everyone had given up on resuscitating him and left the delivery room. One nurse stayed behind, and kept trying. She revived him. He's severely brain damaged, and yet he is a brilliant man. He can do nothing, physically. He uses a speaking device, and types everything with a red dot on his head. His dad hits the output button, and you wouldn't believe what comes out of that man's mind. He is amazing! He lives with his Mom and Dad, Dick and Betty Sanders, who were missionaries in the Chad. He was their third son. They never got any money from the hospital, and never tried to. They refused to hire a lawyer, saying God would take care of their son. When I hear stories like that, sometimes I feel guilty. Their faith out-distanced mine."

"And Dr. Payne kept urging us on, reminding us that we wouldn't always be here to help Daniel, saying we needed to be his advocates now, while we could. So we leaned on the words of Jehoshaphat in 2 Chron. 20:12, 'O God, we do not know what to do, but our eyes are on You!'"

"We eventually hired the lawyer whose name had been given to us by three people. He was a god-send, a trustworthy, fair man with a fabulous reputation. We never did go to court. We settled out-of-court with a lump sum that was put in a trust for Daniel, so he is taken care of financially-speaking."

That financial settlement has enabled Daniel to go to a private, Christian college, which has been the fulfillment of a lifelong dream for him. Years before he was ready to attend college, God provided the means whereby he would be able to do so. Our God of Dreams made sure of that. Thank You, Lord

Jay's dream in process

"He who dwells in the shelter of the Most High will rest... Ps. 91:1

CHAPTER 26

No Matter What Happens

While interviewing Jay, I asked him what he would say to someone who is just beginning the kind of journey he began thirteen years ago. Hesitantly, he responded. "That's a hard question. I'm not one for giving advice. But I would say that the presence of other people who just came alongside was so important. It was helpful when they offered suggestions and helped us do things, but mostly it was their presence, just their reaching out, even when they didn't say anything, that was such a comfort. And of course, God was my greatest comfort. I want to comfort others now in the same way He and other people comforted me."

"And we have to remember that this suffering, even though it goes on day-after-day, month-after-month, year-after-year, is just a short time. This isn't all there is. When we are in heaven, in the throne room with the Lord Jesus, THAT will be forever! Our present sufferings are nothing when compared to the glory and joy and beauty we will experience then (Rom. 8:18)."

"The example given in the Bible by Daniel's three friends, Shadrach, Meshach, and Abednego is my goal. They really didn't think it was very important whether or not they had to suffer. Their focus, their whole purpose in life was to worship the One, True, Living God no matter what happened. What happened didn't matter to them. Whether God chose to save them from the fiery flames in the furnace or not, they knew their God was faithful and would do what was best. Their only desire was to worship Him" (Dan. 3:16-18).

Jay's comments remind me of Charles Spurgeon's words wherein he says that our griefs and sufferings don't really matter, they cannot mar the melody of our praise, but are simply the bass notes of our life song, "To God Be The Glory!"

"It's important to continue to be a pleasing vessel to the Lord and to stay balanced. I want ALL of our children, not just Daniel, to keep walking with the Lord, to be a good testimony for Him."

"So is it necessary," I asked, "to be careful to keep Daniel's injury from consuming your life?"

"Yes. I've enjoyed all the milestones in each of our children's lives as they have grown up. We have fun getting together."

When I asked Jay if God had sent him specific people to help him through these last thirteen years, the names tumbled out quickly with no hesitation.

"I'm afraid I will leave some out, especially those at Emmaus Bible College. God used or is using all these people and many more to bless our lives: Mr. and Mrs. George Nelson, Dennis and Bryan Ford, John and Debbie Kloeppel, my friend Shorti, and Pop Allan, Mr. Gable, Mr. Glock and Jon, John Headrick and his family, Terry and Irene Morgan, Uncle Gary and others. "

"I think a real key for me is those verses in Daniel we talked about earlier. They show me we have to be resolute, determined, if we're going to make it through. We have to keep our hearts on God. It's God all the way. It's God's strength and God exercising faith in us. We have Him and that's Who we take confidence in."

"Hitherto hath the Lord helped us," or, "Thus far the Lord has helped us" (1 Sam. 7:12). That's what we have experienced and what we will experience. It's all about the goodness of the Lord!"

Susan would agree with that. "The story's not finished yet. That's what's so exciting! As things unfold we'll get to see more and more glimpses of God. He is just so unbelievably merciful and gracious! He knows how I am and what I need when I don't even know."

"As the years passed it was a proven fact that whenever I kept my eyes on the Lord there was peace," says Susan. "I was at peace. But it was also a proven fact that when I took my eyes off of the Lord and looked at the storm raging around me, I fell apart. There was one thought in particular that could undo me so badly I literally felt as if I were drowning in fear. I was overwhelmed every time this thought came into my head. It stalked me and plagued me and haunted me. All of God's unfailing faithfulness and abundant provision throughout the years couldn't seem to banish the dread this thought raised in my heart. What's going to happen to Daniel when Jay and I are gone? That thought was so paralyzing that it blotted out my past experiences with God and I simply couldn't handle it. I don't have words to describe the panic that thought set off in me, it was difficult for me to breathe. It put me in a tailspin."

"I would fight that thought with God's Word and prayer as soon as I got enough of a grip on myself to remember to fight it. 'God will make a way… do not fear for I am with you… delight yourself in the Lord… Please God, I can't go there, take that thought from me because I will drive myself crazy if I go there.' Then I would be fine again, leave it and go on. I remember Corrie Ten Boom's comment about the truth that we can trust our unknown future to an all-knowing God. But it was a pervasive, constant battle, more-so than any other one I've ever had."

"About two-years ago, Grant and Jodie called us on the phone and said they had something they needed to talk with us about. Jay and I got on the phone, and Grant said, 'Mom and Dad, we want you to know that when you two are gone, Daniel is ours. We want you to take care of whatever legal things you need to take care of, Dad, so that when you and Mom are gone, we get Daniel. In fact, if you want to get rid of Daniel tomorrow, he's mine. Or whenever you can't handle it anymore, if you can't do it physically or mentally, whatever, we get Daniel.'"

"I can't even think about it without crying. Grant has told us before that he wants his children to know Uncle Daniel because they will be all the richer for knowing him. Before Grant and Jodie were married, he would tell us that next to seeing Jodie he was looking forward to seeing Daniel when he came to our home. God used friends to get Grant and Jodie together when they were each living in different states, and now God has raised up a son-in-law for us to give us peace-of-mind."

"We told our girls more than once that we didn't want Daniel to ever, ever be put in a home to be cared for. They said they would take turns caring for him, but we knew that when it came right down to it they might not choose to or be able to do that."

"But God has given Grant such a heart for Daniel, we are at peace knowing where he will be. God didn't have to do this, but He let me know He had already made provision for Daniel to be cared for in a wonderful, godly Christian home! I mean to say, what a gift!! It's just another huge blessing from the Lord. I sit and think about that and I just marvel at God's provision. It brings tears to my eyes."

"I hesitate to say that – despite God's trustworthiness and proven faithfulness – my fears are all gone. I can't say that when my husband doesn't come home on time I don't start getting scared. I do. Or if I found a lump somewhere in my body I can't say I wouldn't get nervous. I would. But it's different now! Fears, worries, and what-ifs had always been a huge part of my life. But now I can prove that no matter what happens God will see me through it. He has shown Himself to be so kind, loving, strong, faithful, and trustworthy that when something appears to be happening or I'm afraid something is going to happen, I run to Him like David did in Ps. 91. He promises me He will cover me with His feathers and I can take refuge under His wings. He will be with me in trouble"

"One of my biggest fears was of losing a child. I thought that would destroy me. Now I know God will see me through everything. I remember telling a friend while Daniel was in the hospital that I didn't think I would ever smile or be able to live happily again. Now I smile not because of Daniel or his health or his plans to finish college, but because of God. God will get me through, and in Him I will always be okay!"

"I was even able to tell Jodie the week before she got married that my mother's heart would like to pray that God would keep her from suffering. But I couldn't really do that. I told her, 'I will pray for strength for you that your faith and trust in God will remain strong and not fail you, because God will never fail you. I will pray that, no matter what happens, you will throw yourself in your loving Father's Arms and rest in Him until the storm is over, because it's in those times of suffering that we are closest to God. And when we are close to God, no matter what happens, no matter how much we hurt, there's no better place to be."

Amen! And Hallelujah!

Daniel's dream comes true!
Daniel and Joy graduate from Emmaus Bible College on May 7, 2011.

Our God Who Is Presence

"...mostly it was their presence..."

Do you know, dear reader, that Jesus loves you more than you can possibly comprehend or imagine? His Holy Spirit is wooing you this very moment and longing for you to let Him love you and be present in you. The billions of other people who have loved Him down through the ages cannot fill the place in His Heart designed specifically for you. He wants YOUR love. He has made your fingerprints, your voice print, your hair print, and your DNA unique to you. No one else has yours, or ever will have yours, a fact whose reality is beyond your intellectual grasp. You are a unique reflection of God, created by Him in His Image. You are LIKE Him, part of Him. He longs for you to share His life, His grace, His love for you.

Would you be willing, dear reader, to open your life and invite Him in, despite your disbelief or doubts? All the things you dislike about yourself can be given to Him, and He will give you His goodness in exchange for them. Your failures, your guilt, your sins, can be handed-over to Him. He already took all that ugliness to a cross and paid the debt you incurred because of it. You just haven't received the benefits of it yet.

You can tell Him you are tired of living for yourself, and want to start living for Him. You can discover goodness and beauty and joy and peace INSIDE of you, if He lives there. You won't be haunted or plagued by restless dissatisfaction anymore. You will no longer feel a frequent nagging that you don't fit in or belong, or won't get your needs met.

When you are weary, He offers rest. When you are grieved, He offers forgiveness and freedom. When you are dull, He offers fresh ideas and creative possibilities. When you are tired of living, He gives new zest for life. When you are bored, He offers stimulating conversation like no other. When you are confused, He provides clarity. When you need a hearty laugh, He'll give you one. He meets your every need.

Too good to be true? Indeed, by all our human standards, He is too good to be true. Recall the most stunningly beautiful sight you have ever seen. It pales in comparison to Him. Recall the greatest thrill of your life. Relationship with Him exceeds it. Remember your deepest ecstasy. He's deeper still. Think about your gravest desperation. He could have rescued you from that, and probably did without your awareness of it.

He's always near you, because He loves you. He's waiting for you. Remember the time you were tempted to do something you knew in your "better-self" you didn't really want to do? You did it anyway, and liked yourself a little less because of it. We don't have within ourselves the strength to do what's right, what's best for us. God gives us the strength we need to win those battles with temptation.

If your intellect is in your way, tell it to read "The Case For Christ" by Lee Strobel, or "More Than A Carpenter" by Josh McDowell, former atheists whose intellects discovered there were far greater realities than their puny little capabilities could grasp. Our intellects fail us, just like everything and everybody, sooner or later.

Let Jesus in. Take the risk. Give your failures, weaknesses, and sins to Him. Tell Him you can't make it on your own. Our Father God knew that when He created you. That's why He asked Jesus to become a man - for <u>YOU</u>! Then God the Holy Spirit will take the little trust and understanding you have now and grow it very large indeed, just as He has for Susan, Jay, and Daniel.

If you don't know what to say, maybe this would do. "Oh, Jesus, I need YOU. I want to let You love me. I need Your strength, Your comfort, Your clarity, Your forgiveness, Your everything. You created me and know what's best for me. I give You my "wrong-ness", my selfishness, my sins in exchange for Your right-ness. I don't want them anymore. I give You control of my life. Help me to break through the limits of my intellect. Don't let me be like the scientist who knows You are real but refuses to bow down to anyonc, and so lives as if You are not real. Help me to bash my pride. Help me to yield to You. Do that work in me, Father God, Jesus Christ, and Holy Spirit. Teach me what it means to have You present inside me as my Father, my Savior, my Friend, my Teacher, my Comforter, my All-In-All. Show me that I am precious, and honored in Your sight, and how much You have to offer me. I count on that, dear God."

In Jesus' Name, Amen!

And Hallelujah!

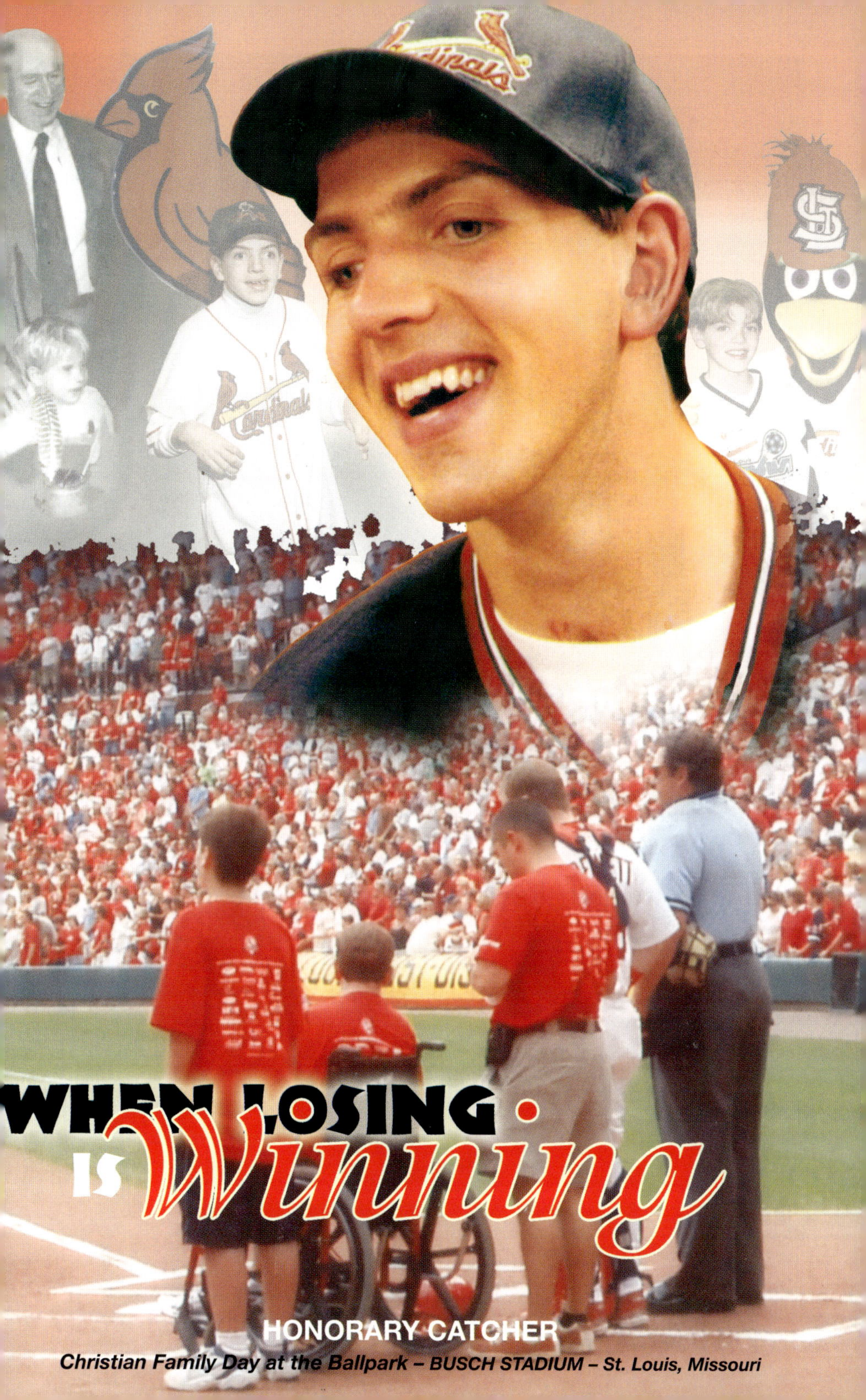
WHEN LOSING IS Winning
HONORARY CATCHER
Christian Family Day at the Ballpark – BUSCH STADIUM – St. Louis, Missouri

First Birthday!

Christmas Morning Surprise

Fred Bird, Daniel, and friend, Jay Moline

St. Louis Blues players skating with Daniel

Busch Stadium usher, John, Daniel, and Jodie

Soccer – his first love!

Playing baseball

8th grade
graduation banquet
Word of Life
Christian School

CMN Telethon with Steve and Sandy Sanders, Ozzie Smith, and News Anchor Cree

Visit from Harlem Globetrotter after third open heart surgery.

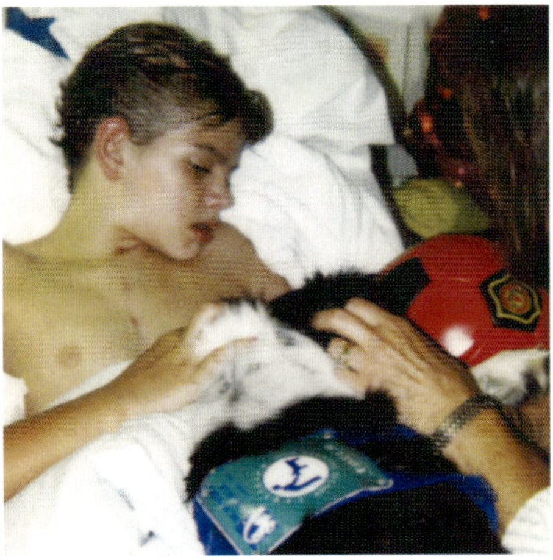

Visit from Mary Ann and Scivvies (support dog)

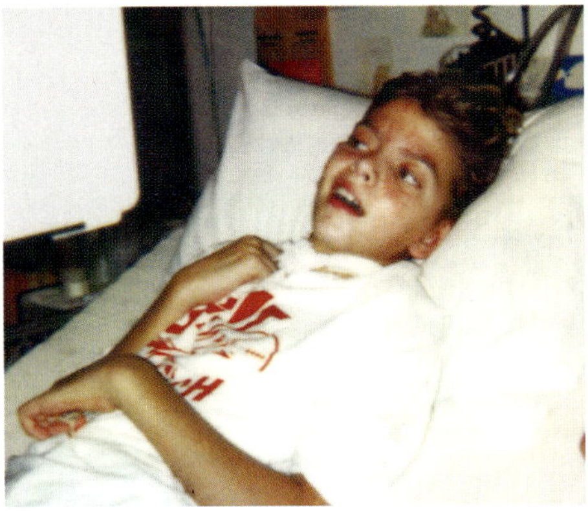

First Smile!

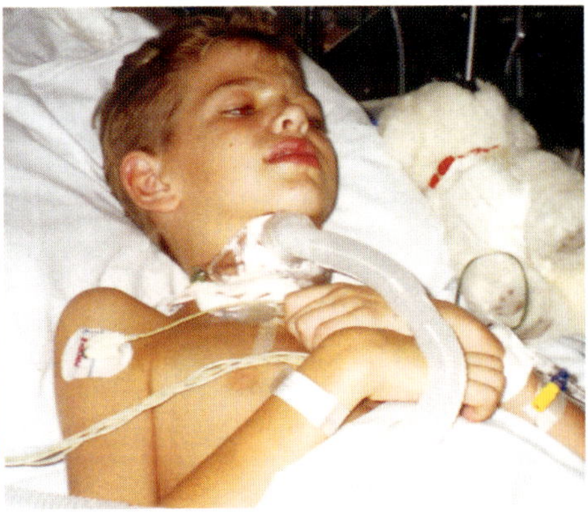

Fighting for his life while on ventilator

Adeli Suit Therapists in Miami, Florida

Daniel at Busch Stadium
"Blast It Out of Busch""

Dolphin therapy in Key Largo, Florida

Groomsman in OT Tracy Coleman's wedding

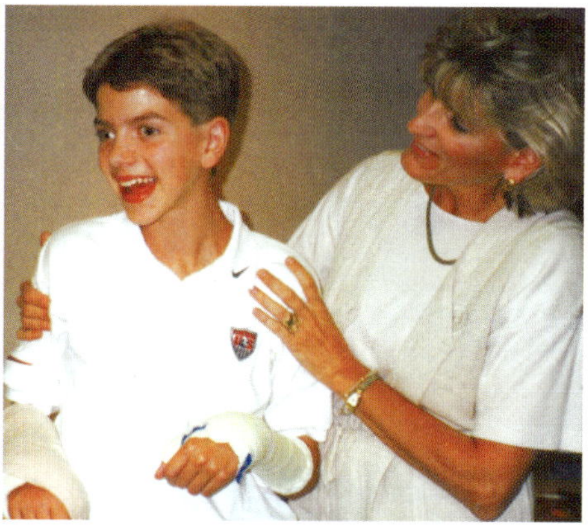

13th birthday party

KPLR News Anchor and friend,
Christine Buck

Having fun in an airplane Uncle Jim is flying

St. Louis Cardinals shortstop, Ozzie Smith

A gift from friend Jon Glock:
a signed Titan's jersey

Getting ready for high school

Emmaus Bible College graduation
with sister Joy

Daniel at Christmas with Seth and Adam Hutcherson, Jayme, Jodie and JoyAnn

Daniel with Jordan, Parker and Arial at Disneyland

Daniel and Chris Boyer

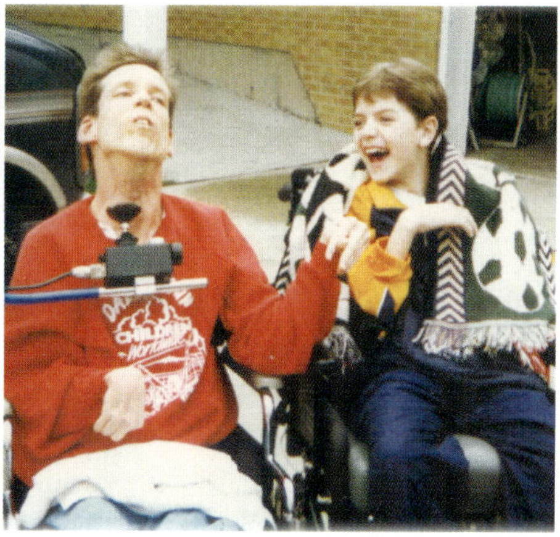

Having fun with Brad Sanders

Daniel and Jon Glock

Daniel and Jayme

Shorti Cribb, Dad, and Daniel at Emmaus Bible College Senior Banquet

Matt Airey, college friend

5k Race with Bart and Tracy Coleman

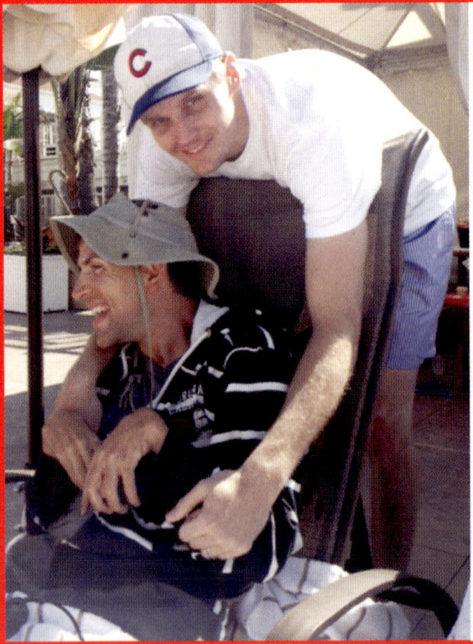

Daniel with brother-in-law and best friend, Grant Botma

Talking baseball with nephew Parker

The *Daniel* Project

Individuals and families who live with disabilities need the encouragement and vision available in this book. It has much to offer both those who already know God and those who have not yet recognized Him at work in their lives. It also offers help to all who are hurting for any reason whatsoever. If you know of anyone who might be blessed by this book, we invite you to participate in The Daniel Project. All proceeds from The Daniel Project and sales of this book will go to Joni and Friends, an international ministry serving people and families with disabilities.

If you know anyone with disabilities of any kind, pass one on to them.

Look for folks with disabilities when you go shopping, eat in restaurants, attend fairs or festivals, and hand one to them.

Visit hospitals with children's units and pass them out to parents. Give them to people in waiting rooms and visitors in intensive-care units.

Tell others on Facebook and Twitter how the book impacted you.

Give a case to merchants to put on their counter to resell to customers.

Buy a case to distribute at regional meetings and associations for those who live with disabilities.

Pass them out at your church, at support group meetings and Bible Studies.

Give the book to friends, even strangers, as a gift.

<u>When Losing Is Winning</u> is available through
the Stratman Family at:
whenlosingiswinning.book@gmail.com

Glorifying God!

Our God of Mysterious Ways

For over thirty-four years Joni and Friends has been dedicated to extending the love and message of Christ to people who are affected by disability, including not only the disabled person, but also family members and friends. Their objective is to meet the physical, emotional, and spiritual needs of these folks in practical ways. Their web-site address is www.joniandfriends.org and their phone number is 818-707-5664.

Joni Eareckson Tada, the founder and chief executive officer of Joni and Friends International Disabilities Center, is an international advocate for people with disabilities. A diving accident in 1967 left Joni Eareckson, then 17, a quadriplegic in a wheelchair. After two years of rehabilitation, she emerged with new skills and a fresh determination to help others in similar situations. She founded Joni and Friends in 1979 to provide Christ-centered programs to special needs families, as well as training to churches. Through the organization's *Christian Institute on Disability*, Joni and her team have helped develop disability ministry courses of study in major Christian universities and seminaries, including Dallas Theological Seminary. It's Mrs. Tada's hope to ignite a passion among many more young people to reach people with disabilities and their families around the world for Christ.

Joni and Friends has many ministry arms, one of which is Family Retreats. My husband Tom has served at twenty-six of these retreats, called by God via Joni's radio ministry in 1996 as he drove home from work one wintry afternoon. Tom's excitement that afternoon, generated by Joni's call for volunteers to serve at Family Retreats, was matched by mine, generated by the same radio program as I listened to it in our home that same afternoon. I had experienced an excitement, an urging, a drawing to the retreats also, not for myself, but for my husband, who was serving as a speech pathologist in the Princeton School District and had time available in the summer to serve at Family Retreats.

Tom's role in the Princeton Schools involved working with students who had multiple disabilities, including parents and teachers, to create a way for them to communicate with each other. Many students were non-verbal, and Tom facilitated ways for them to interact with the environment around them. His ministry as a speech pathologist had prepared him well for service at Joni Retreats. We both knew it, and experienced God's call for him to become involved.

When Tom returned from his first Family Retreat in Pennsylvania, he knew he would go again the following year and take our twelve-year-old daughter with him. Kathleen didn't want to go to the Joni Retreat, but Tom assured her that if she did not enjoy the experience she would not have to return again. Kathleen was so greatly blessed that summer by the families and volunteers at Retreat, she returned to serve at twelve additional retreats in the following nine years. Family Retreats became part of the warp and woof of our lives.

When Tom retired from the Princeton Schools after twenty-nine years, we prayed together, asking God what He would like us to do with the rest of our lives, whether those years be few or many.

In recent years, God had shown us that Eph. 2:10, "For you are God's workmanship, created in Christ Jesus to do good works which He has prepared in advance for you," was not just His perspective for our younger years, but was relevant right up to the moment of our death. Retirement was simply a "freeing up" of more hours in which to glorify Him and serve His people in a different way than we had previously served.

God led us, two lifetime city-dwellers, in His mysterious ways, into a ministry beyond our wildest imaginings. We purchased forty acres of land from my cousin, Ethel, who lived with her husband on a farm in Kentucky. I had fallen in love with the lush, green, rolling hills of Alexandria as a child when my parents would "visit the country" where my Aunt Louise and Uncle Eddy lived on a hundred-acre farm, lovely like Pooh Bear's "Hundred-acre wood" of Christopher Robin's childhood days. Through the years Ethel and her husband Kenny had become my spiritual mentors and later, Tom's as well.

Tom and I built a log home, inspired by one in which Ethel's son, Gerry, and his wife, Carol, lived with their three wonderful sons. Settled in the country, we felt truly blessed, unaware of all God was working out for us behind the scenes.

One day in April at our church, a young girl of fourteen years approached me with the startling question, "Would you like to buy my filly, Mrs. Reynolds?" Mouth agape, I stared at her. She proceeded to tell me her family was moving to Vermont, she had raised Willow from birth, and didn't want to sell her to someone she didn't know. When I asked her "Why me?" she responded, "I know you would take good care of her." I told J'Lynn I had never had a horse, nor had my husband, and we had only ridden a few times. Undaunted by my "I can't believe you asked" response, she waited for my answer.

"Let me talk with my husband and pray about it," I replied.

Later that afternoon, Tom, our then seventeen-year-old daughter, Kathleen, and I prayed, asking God if He was directing us to buy this horse. Over the next few days of continuing prayer, it became clear to us He was indeed so doing.

With anxious anticipation, we began reading voraciously about horses and their care. Tom fenced in an acre of land for her, and in May, J'Lynn and her daddy delivered Willow to our doorstep. What a beauty she was! One-year-old, a brown and white and black paint, sweet and gentle, she came when we called her and spent her days romping in the pasture above our house. Many times each day I'd look out the window to see how she and the goat we bought to keep her company were faring. Daily she was fussed-over and groomed. We fell in love quickly, Willow and Tom and I.

As new horse owners, Tom and I decided to take riding lessons twice a week at a nearby farm, knowing Willow would be ready to train and ride in one year's time. We became comfortable, somewhat experienced, and quite happy with our new role as horse lovers. We began seeking God in prayer about His plans for us relative to horses. We knew He had a much bigger, more significant plan in bringing Willow to us than we could presently perceive.

Shortly after we purchased Willow, the yearly letter arrived from Joni and Friends Retreat in Chicago, describing the scheduled activities for the Family Retreat Tom and Kathleen would attend in June, 2001. For the first time at the Oakwood Inn Retreat, one of the activities included an evening of horseback riding for folks with disabilities. The Holy Spirit highlighted that for us, we felt a gentle prodding, and began asking God if the horses in our life were to include ones to take to the Joni and Friends Retreats. Late in June when Tom and Kathleen came home from serving at the Retreat, Tom described the long lines of folks waiting to ride the horses, and the excitement generated by their presence. He also described the disappointment of those folks, both adults and children, who had been unable to ride because the time allotted ended before their turn came.

Knowing we were being nudged by God to do so, we began looking into what was needed for us to take horses to some of the retreats so all who attended would have the opportunity to ride. Novices that we were and knowing the kind of God we serve, we anticipated a daunting adventure.

The next week as we exited the feed store where we purchased grain for Willow, we stopped to look at the local bulletin board, as we usually did. For the first time, and providentially so, we noted a "volunteers needed" sign for workers at a nearby farm that provided equestrian therapy for folks with disabilities. We were not interested in providing therapy, but in providing recreation for riders at the Joni and Friends Family Retreats. But the direction of the Spirit was clear, we signed up to serve, and another chapter in our challenging adventure began. We learned to help the riders with disabilities mount the horses, we walked alongside to enable them to remain astride, we led the horses when needed, and helped with therapeutic activities during the rides. New insights, new experiences, new joys were savored by us, including Tom, who had already worked so many years with folks with disabilities.

Because Willow was so young, we knew we could not take her to Family Retreats. We needed horses that were older, settled, unflappable, "bomb-proof". As we began inquiring, we received many cautions about the typical pitfalls that greenhorns such as we encounter when purchasing horses. Horses with bad habits that weren't readily observable, and lame horses who were drugged so their limp was not apparent, were two of the most common problems about which we were warned. Daunted and overwhelmed at the thought of wading into unknown waters, we went to the Lord and asked for His guidance and direction.

The next week at our riding lesson we mentioned our search for horses to Anna, our teacher. She said, "The horse you use during your lessons is excellent for that kind of riding. She meets all the necessary requirements. I can sell her to you for twenty-two-hundred dollars." God's plan, laid out so clearly in Anna's offer, was astonishing. God was not requiring us who knew nothing to go looking for horses. He was bringing them to us! He was calling us, the unequipped, to serve Him, but He was equipping us! My heart smiled as I remembered a wise, elderly lady once telling me, "God doesn't always call the equipped, but He always equips the called!"

I was riding Callie in my lessons precisely because I told Anna I was inexperienced and needed a safe, gentle, quiet horse. I had been riding her twice weekly for many months. Tom and I were thrilled, and went home praising God for His provision!

When we went to our next lesson Anna told us she had been thinking about it, and decided she could not let us have Callie because she was such a good brood mare. She had given Anna five foals, all of whom brought an excellent price at auction. We were disappointed, but we knew God had a plan. We told Anna we understood, and went home to ask the Lord for clarity. The next day Anna called and said she wasn't at peace and knew God was telling her to sell Callie to us. And she did! Anna also helped us find a pony for the children and small adults to ride. Callie was a quarter horse and just right for adults but too large for children.

As the owners of three horses, we needed to make pastureland out of some of our forested acres. With the help of friends and family, we cut down approximately two hundred trees, some very small, some quite large, to make a pasture on the wooded hillsides for Callie, Cassie, and Willow.

A truck and trailer to haul the horses to the retreats were the next items on our "equipping" list. We had never driven a truck, so much research was needed before we could even begin inquiring about them. Within weeks our Jehovah-Jireh (Hebrew for "our God who provides") led us to both the trailer and truck He had waiting for us.

God's faithfulness in providing unflagging courage enabled us to negotiate the most anxiety-ridden, fear-filled part yet to come on our adventure. I'll never forget the many hours I watched in admiration as my mild-mannered, laid-back husband, who had driven a small Toyota Tercel for the previous ten years, with gritted teeth, clenched jaw, and a prayer on his lips, practiced parking our seemingly monstrous, fourteen-foot, fifth-wheel horse trailer in a large abandoned grocery store lot. I remember the first time, with horses loaded in the trailer, grim determination, and pure grit, he began his first trek up and down the winding, narrow, two-laned back roads leading from our graveled driveway to the highway many miles away. Kathleen and I followed him in a seventeen-foot U-Haul truck filled with hay, a portable corral, feed and everything we needed to make a temporary home for horses at the Retreat. We found ourselves doing things we never dreamed nor imagined we'd be doing. God's plans are so much bigger than our dreams! God brought us a young man named Daniel Frasure to accompany us to the Retreats and help us with the horses. His diligence, sense of responsibility and positive attitude were a great blessing to us.

And then came the joy! Ah, such joy - the thrill, the blessing of working with folks with disabilities, many of whom had never ridden before, as they struggled to mount the horses and experienced the delight and satisfaction of a new or rare occurrence in their lives. So much courage, such perseverance! Isaiah, who was non-verbal, severely limited physically, and wheelchair-bound from cerebral palsy, talked his mother into wheeling him over to the horses three times before he finally mustered up the courage to give it a try. Lydia, five-years-old, who was totally paralyzed and able to move only her eyelids, blinked twice to let her parents know she did indeed want to ride the pony. Jill, severely crippled, with easily-broken, brittle bones from progressive arthritis and unable to ride, sat in her wheelchair and petted Cassie, her radiant smile rivaling the sunset on the hillside. These, and many like them, were people who inspired me, who reminded me how great were my own physical blessings, who elicited admiration and provoked humility in me. For the next three years we were privileged to haul our horses to six retreats. Our oldest rider was seventy and our youngest was two-years-old.

Then physical limitations began to assert themselves in my life. Osteoarthritis, chrondromalacia, and bone spurs on my knees began to limit my ability to walk the hilly pastures of home and care for our horses. The chores Tom and I had enjoyed doing together became burdensome for Tom to do alone. He noticed his energy level was no longer what it had been before he retired. A back injury laid him low for many weeks. And so, after much prayer and discussion, we decided it was time to let go of the Hallelujah Horse Ministry, which had evolved delightfully and now included hauling our pony, Cassie, to Vacation Bible School and a local nursing home.

Selling Willow was difficult for us. She was our "baby", now four years old, and Tom's consistent choice when he and I took our rides on country roads together. We had no idea how to proceed in finding a new home for her with someone who would love and care for this gentle, sweet-natured beauty. We called J'Lynn, the young lady who had sold her to us three years earlier, to ask her what she thought would be a "fair" price to ask, and how to proceed in the process of selling her. J'Lynn's response to our questions was incredible and exactly what we needed.

"Oh, Mrs. Reynolds, I want to buy her back! We have farmland now. I have been looking for just the right horse for our family and I want her back! I will pay what you ask and pay to have her shipped here to Vermont!" I stood rooted to the spot, my heart pounding with joy as I praised our faithful God Who goes before us and makes the way for us, not only in very great trials but also in little tiny problems such as this, long before we even know there will be a problem! How deeply loving and solicitous He is, how marvelous His mysterious ways!

Selling Willow and our other horses changed the face of our ministry with Joni and Friends. God returned Tom to his previous position as a one-on-one volunteer for a person with disabilities. I became Family Coordinator and began using more extensively the writing gifts He had entrusted to me since my days as a teenager.

Meanwhile, in various and sundry but equally marvelous ways, God continues to raise up thousands of volunteers every summer in many states and overseas as well. Amazing people haul their speed boats and skis, tubes and pontoons, canoes and fishing gear to Family Retreat sites where thousands of amazing families with disabilities experience God's love as they have the opportunity to try new things they've never done before. They see God's love shining in the eyes of the volunteers, they savor the inclusiveness that comes with being surrounded by other families who are "just like us," who warmly commiserate instead of starkly staring. They return home restored, renewed, refreshed, ready to continue the arduous journey our heavenly Father has marked out for them because He knows what's best for each of us.

Come join us, share in the journey as volunteer or attendee as we continue to marvel at the Self-revelation of our grand and glorious God of Mysterious Ways! Thank You, Lord!

Notes:

[1]Harriet Beecher Stowe, *How To Live On Christ*, (a little booklet)

[2]Fanny J. Crosby, To God Be The Glory (Carol Stream, IL: Tabernacle Publishing Co., 1989)

[3]Charles Spurgeon, Morning By Morning, p.133 (New Kensington, PA: Whitaker House 1985, 2001)

[4]The "Psalty" tape adapted, The Singing Songbook by Adam Whitley, Psalty's Kids Co.
Ernie and Debbie Rettino, The Cares Chorus, Maranatha! Music/Word, 1985.

[5]C.S. Lewis, The Four Loves, p. 191 (New York, NY; Inspirational Press, 1994)

[6]Joni Eareckson Tada, The God I Love, p. 209 (Grand Rapids, MI: Zondervan 2003)

[7]E. Michael and Sharon Rusten, The One Year Book Of Christian History, p. 214 (Wheaton, IL: Tyndale House Publishers, Inc. 2003)

[8]Hudson Taylor - Source unknown

[9]E. Michael and Sharon Rusten, The One Year Book Of Christian History, p. 74 (Wheaton, IL: Tyndale House Publishers, Inc. 2003)

[10]Ibid. p. 75

[11]Jan Karon, These High, Green Hills, p. 301 (Colorado Springs, CO: Lion Publishing, 1996)

[12]James Strong, Strong's Exhaustive Concordance Of The Bible, p. 33 (Nashville, TN: Thomas Nelson Publishers, 1990)

[13]Merriam-Webster, Webster's Ninth New Collegiate Dictionary, (Springfield, MA: Merriam-Webster Inc., 1986)

[14]Mrs. Charles E. Cowman, Streams In The Desert, May 10th (Urichsville, OH: Barbour Publishing, 1965)

[15]George MacDonald, The Parish Papers p. 223, (Colorado Springs, CO: Chariot Victor Pub., 1997)

[16]C.S. Lewis, The Weight Of Glory, p. 14 (San Francisco, CA: Harper Collins Pub., 2001)

[17]Edwin McNeill Poteat, Source unknown, Clergyman and Educator, 1861-1937

[18]God Will Make A Way, words and music by Don Moen, 1990, Integrity's Hosanna! Music

[19]Catherine Marshall, A Man Called Peter, (New York, NY: McGraw-Hill 1951)

[20]Samuel Dowse Robbins, Daily Strength For Daily Needs, p. 83 (Boston, New York, Toronto, London: A Bullfinch Press Book, Little, Brown and Company, 1994)

Zephaniah 3:17 adapted from The Jerusalem Bible, (Garden City NY: Doubleday & Co. Inc. 1966)

We beg your understanding for sources we were unable to locate or contact.